PRAI
CULTUR

MU01075492

"*Cultura & Cash* isn't just a book; it's an intuitive and practical approach to helping you unlearn thinking that doesn't serve you and expand you into the rich bitch you deserve to become. This guidebook will serve as your trusted financial bestie, guiding you towards financial freedom and a legacy that's uniquely yours."

—**Vanessa Santos**, partner and co-CEO #WeAllGrow Latina

"Gigi's *Cultura & Cash* is a game-changer for first-gen Latinas like me. It's like having a trusted friend by your side, guiding you through the maze of finances with cultural understanding. If you're ready to unlock your financial potential while embracing your heritage, this book is your key!"

—**Marivette Navarrete**, founder, The Mujerista

"Giovanna's wisdom, charisma, and genuine desire to help others shine through every page. I wholeheartedly recommend *Cultura & Cash* to anyone, especially first-generation individuals, seeking to take control of their finances, embrace their cultural heritage, and chart a path toward financial freedom."

—**Jannese Torres**, award-winning Latina money expert and host of *Yo Quiero Dinero*

"As a first gen Latina who has been able to break out of generational cycles, one of the biggest relationships I needed to fix was my relationship with money. In this book, Gigi provides readers with a much-needed perspective on starting and maintaining generational wealth while understanding cultural implications one doesn't usually find in traditional financial education content."

—**Katya Echazarreta**, activist and first Mexican-born woman in space

"*Cultura & Cash* helps our first-generation comunidad understand how culture shapes our current mindset with money along with the tangible ways to shift towards a more positive and impactful relationship con dinero! Thank you, Gigi, for helping Latinos build wealth."

—**Patricia Mota**, president and CEO, Hispanic Alliance for Career Enhancement, and cofounder, SHENIX®

"*Cultura & Cash* will change the game for first gen young people seeking to transform generational cycles of financial insecurity into financial freedom. Financial trauma is a visceral part of the first gen experience, and Gigi has written a book that is empowering, unflinching, and long overdue."

—**Alejandra Campoverdi**, national bestselling author of *First Gen: A Memoir*

"Gigi's voice and message are so necessary in the financial literacy landscape right now. She is providing a financial road map so many of us lack when we are the 'firsts' in our communities. This book is the perfect way to help you take charge of your finances and start building wealth—not someday but right now."

—**Mandi Woodruff-Santos**, founder, MandiMoney Makers Career Academy, and cohost, Brown Ambition podcast

"FINALLY! A finance book that gives you a real-life look into what it takes to build wealth as a first-generation American. *Cultura & Cash* not only guides you on the path from starting with very little to securing your financial future, but it also offers advice for navigating challenging money discussions within your family. If you're seeking practical financial tips from a financial expert who doesn't sugarcoat things, get this book!"

—**Janet Escobar**, author of *The Latina Trailblazer*

"Cultura & Cash goes beyond traditional personal finance advice by addressing issues that are unique to the first gen experience. It covers everything from paying off debt and investing to financially supporting—and setting boundaries with—our loved ones and helping our parents plan for their retirement. This thoughtful, honest, and refreshing book is just what our comunidad needs."

—**Cindy Zuniga-Sanchez**, author, speaker, and founder of Zero-Based Budget Coaching LLC

"Gigi gets me, and she gets our comunidad. This isn't just another book about making money. It's about shifting our perspective on how to build wealth without compromising our cultural values."

—**Alejandra Aguirre**, owner and co-founder, Cadena Collective

"Gio always delivers financial literacy online *sin pelos en la lengua*, or without holding back, and this book does not fall short. To have someone speak to personal finance education in cultural context is a big deal for the Latino community. This book provides specific challenges first gen Latinos come across when it comes to navigating money, and how Giovanna recommends navigating them, leveraging her expertise and experience. It's the intersection of book smarts and cultural smarts we've been looking for."

—**Lyanne Alfaro**, host of the *Moneda Moves* podcast

"*Cultura & Cash* is a fantastic place to start your money journey. The book breaks down practical steps the reader can implement to take charge of their financial wellness. As a first gen immigrant, I'm a fan!"

—**Jamila Souffrant**, author of *Your Journey to Financial Freedom* and host of the *Journey to Launch* podcast

"*Cultura & Cash* is the practical money guide you need to get your money right and secure your financial future with family in mind."

—**Farnoosh Torabi,** financial expert and author of
A Healthy State of Panic

CULTURA &CASH

CULTURA

&CASH

LESSONS FROM
THE FIRST GEN MENTOR
FOR MANAGING FINANCES &
CULTURAL EXPECTATIONS

GIOVANNA GONZÁLEZ

FAST
COMPANY
Press

Fast Company Press
New York, New York
www.fastcompanypress.com

This work is being published under the Fast Company Press imprint by an exclusive arrangement with *Fast Company*. *Fast Company* and the *Fast Company* logo are registered trademarks of Mansueto Ventures, LLC. The Fast Company Press logo is a wholly owned trademark of Mansueto Ventures, LLC.

Distributed by River Grove Books

Design and composition by Greenleaf Book Group
Cover design by Greenleaf Book Group
Illustrations by Alyssa Gonzalez

Publisher's Cataloging-in-Publication data is available.

Print ISBN: 978-1-63908-076-2

eBook ISBN: 978-1-63908-077-9

First Edition

For my Aunt Patty, who always said, "You should write a book about that!" And for my Nana, who is the reason I have a better life in the US. Las quiero mucho.

CONTENTS

WELCOME TO YOUR RICH-GIRL ERA

Money allows me to live a life I love.

"I want to be better with money, but I don't know where to start."

"I know I have to get my finances together, but money feels scary to me."

"No matter what I do with my money, I can't seem to get ahead."

"I work so hard for my money, but I don't know where it all goes."

These are all a sampling of comments I get from my financial literacy workshop students or even the comment section on my social media accounts. Most people who say this often feel they don't have a good understanding of how money works and are intimidated by all they have to learn to get better. If this is you, it's not your fault!

Nobody Teaches Us This Stuff

Nobody teaches us how money works. It's not taught to us at school, and if you have immigrant parents like me, it likely wasn't taught to you at home.

To make matters worse, the money advice that is out there can be outdated and unrelatable. "Skip Starbucks and make your coffee at home to save money!" or "Work a part-time job during college to avoid student debt!" On what planet?! This old-school money advice just doesn't work in this day and age.

Financial literacy is riddled with confusing financial jargon. There are formulas, new acronyms, and math involved. Learning money education as a beginner can feel intimidating when you don't know the industry lingo, and it can leave you feeling small or incapable of doing better. Traditional money advice is known for using finger-wagging tactics and judges you for not knowing what you didn't know. It doesn't feel like a safe space to learn. When you only see white, cis, male financial pundits talking about money, it's easy to feel like money management is not for you and that it's only something "white people do." What does a middle-aged white man know about my specific life needs as a First Gen Latina? He doesn't share my struggles or my worries.

No wonder you've never learned!

Money Matters

But that ends with this book because money affects us all. Understanding how to use money effectively is an important life skill that affects every aspect of your life, including where you live, what you eat, and what type of healthcare you have access to. Having money allows you to show up for family and those you love when they need it. Money gives you the means to have experiences that will enrich your life and buy things that bring you joy. Money brings you financial peace and can preserve your mental health during life's ups and downs. Money gives you options and allows you to live the life you deserve, which is why I'm going to teach you how it works.

My Journey from Financially Broke to Money Expert

As a Latina financial educator and finfluencer, I make financial concepts easy to understand. As a speaker, I've taught financial literacy topics like budgeting, credit building, and investing to nonprofits, employee resource groups, universities, and thousands of students at various colleges. As a content creator, I make edutaining videos that explain money basics like how to open a Roth IRA or how to pay off debt to my social media community of 225,000-plus followers. I love talking about all things money, especially with First Gen and other women of color.

Although I'm considered an expert now, my money journey started similar to yours: broke, confused, and not having a clue on where to start. When I felt ready to learn, I turned to books to teach myself. I started reading all the money books I could get my hands on—well over fifty books! I bought books online, borrowed books from friends, and checked out books from my local library. I felt like Belle in *Beauty and the Beast*—reading the same books over and over for fun.

I read some of the classics like *Rich Dad Poor Dad* and *Automatic Millionaire*. I read books by well-known financial experts like Suze Orman and David Bach. These books taught me all the fundamentals, like how to budget, tackle debt, and start investing—all things I knew nothing about when I started my money journey. After reading those books, I finally understood the meaning of all these new acronyms and financial terms, like APR and FICO score. I felt like I'd cracked the code and had mastered a new language: the language of money.

A shift happened inside me. Instead of tuning out at the first mention of money talk, I'd lean in and ask more questions. Money didn't feel scary anymore. It felt like something that was within reach and available to me too. I felt confident and like I finally had the knowledge and tools I needed to tackle my finances and make smarter money moves. I was eager to get off the struggle bus and transform my finances for the better.

When Two Money Cultures Clash

But what I experienced instead was a complete culture clash with my family. In the books I read, there was no mention of how to navigate finances and cultural expectations with an immigrant family. Since I wasn't given any guidance, I winged it and followed the traditional money advice from the books I'd been reading. Some of this advice included, "Don't lend money to friends or family. You're not a bank!" or "To trim your budget as much as you can, stop eating out at restaurants!" Those books taught me that if I wanted to improve my money situation, the only way to do it was by prioritizing my own money goals above all else.

This is what it looked like. When my family wanted me to invite them out to a nice restaurant and foot the bill, I would say, "I can't afford to pay for us to go to a restaurant because I'm on a budget." Or when I got a phone call asking me to pay for an unexpected surgery cost, I said, "No, I can't charge that on my credit card because I don't have the money to pay it." Other times I would feel guilty for not being more giving and would cave to the pressure just to appease my family. But it usually threw my budget off track, which set me back financially and left me feeling frustrated.

Nothing could have prepared me for the tsunami of backlash and heartache I'd receive from family for putting into practice what I've learned. I was called selfish, "una mal agradecida," a "coda," and out of touch with my roots for saying no to family when they needed money. This was so hurtful and caught me by complete surprise. Why was my family being so tough on me? I was just trying to be a financially responsible adult. Didn't they get it? Didn't they want me to make better money choices? All I wanted was to be a good daughter—granddaughter—and be financially successful. Could I not be all three?

Those Other Books Weren't Written for Us

I eventually realized I was struggling with money and family because I was trying to implement financial advice I'd learned from mostly white male authors. White male authors write from an American, individualistic point of view. The values that are held in high regard to American individualism are being independent and self-reliant, and pulling yourself up by the bootstraps.

That means that if you get yourself into a financial pickle, you figure out how to get out of it alone. You don't ask for "handouts;" you don't ask others for help. American individualism encourages you to put your needs before someone else's, with the thinking being that everyone is responsible for their own financial situation. Every man for himself.

This could not be more different from what is expected and accepted in my household. My family's Mexican values follow more of a collectivist society, where they take pride in tapping into community when facing financial hardship. Money is communal, it's there to help us all. It's not embarrassing to ask for money. As a matter of fact, it shows how loved you are. People trust and love you so much that they're willing to loan or gift you their hard-earned money when you need it. They're willing to go into debt for you. There is no bigger badge of pride. As an individual, you're expected to put your needs aside and do what's best for the group. Even if it's at your expense. The group's needs are always more important than yours.

No wonder I was struggling! I was navigating two completely different money cultures—a perfect example of when book smarts don't work in real life.

Traditional personal finance books left me hanging. How is it possible that I'd read dozens of money books and yet hadn't received any tools on how to navigate finances with my immigrant family? Why didn't they explain that different money cultures exist and that there isn't just "one way" to handle money? Why didn't any of those writers teach me how to budget financial support for my family, set financial boundaries, or help me plan for my parents' retirement? These are all issues that affect our community and our dinero, and I'd been left completely unprepared.

Why I Wrote This Book

The truth is simple: White men like Dave Ramsey or Tony Robbins don't have our lived experience. They don't know what it's like to be expected to chip in money for their distant cousin's quinceñera when you can hardly afford your own rent. Nobody is hitting them up, asking them to cosign on a car loan for their uncle with no credit. They've never had to deal with any of that. These writers can't speak, teach, or write about something they haven't lived through. They simply don't have the cultural nuance or lived experience to show us how to navigate money as bicultural Latinas.

The First Gen money experience is different, and I understand it. That's why I wrote *Cultura & Cash*. As a First Gen Latina, I've experienced firsthand the stress, pressure, and hardship that comes from handling two clashing money cultures.

We are left completely on our own to manage money and debt with little to no financial knowledge. We feel the pressure of making something out of ourselves and making our family proud. We don't just go into adulthood and forget about others. We are much more family oriented. Our families are important to us, and we want to bring them with us on our financial journey. We want to uplift our parents, siblings, and any other extended family who rallied around to help get us where we are today.

For a lot of us, helping out financially is how we show respect and gratitude for those who gave so much to us. But doing all this while juggling significant student debt and having no other financial support is not easy. We don't get a blueprint. We want to financially support those we love without leaving ourselves behind. This is why we need a book that addresses the unique challenges our community faces.

A Money Book for First Gen by First Gen

Not only have I lived through the hardships, but I'm also happy to share that I've come out on the other side. Through years of lived experience, I've finally found the right balance of both money cultures that allows me to build financial prosperity for myself and future generations while also looking back and financially supporting my family. My philosophy is to pick and choose the best of both worlds. Hold on to the best from the American money culture and the best from your immigrant parents' money culture to find the balance that works well for you. That's one of the best parts of being First Gen—being exposed to two ways of doing things.

Now, I can give freely to my family in a way that's in alignment with my budget and my values. And sometimes that means saying "No" or "Not right now." Now, I give money to my family not out of fear, guilt, or a sense of obligation but out of a place of empowerment and gratitude for those who raised me. And let me tell you, the latter feels so much better.

Is This Book Only for First Gen?

In case the title didn't give it away, *Cultura & Cash* was unapologetically written for the First Gen community, specifically First Gen Latinas. They are who I want to reach and leave a mark on. My goal with this book is to pave the way for Latinas who come after me by sharing personal anecdotes recounting the lessons I've learned along the way.

Since this book centers the First Gen experience, you'll find a sprinkle of Spanglish throughout the book and see me refer to common Latine dichos and beliefs you can relate to. This book was written for you! Cultura & Cash is the culturally relevant book I wish I'd had as a young adult navigating money for the first time.

But this isn't to say others can't benefit from the knowledge in this book. If you're a fellow woman of color but don't identify as a First Gen Latina, I see you and am rooting for your success too. I know you'll still gain a lot from the content in this book.

A few years ago, I was very impacted by Minda Harts's career book, *The Memo*. Minda didn't write that book for me. As a Black woman, she wrote it for Black women. I know because she explicitly said it in the introduction, similar to how I'm doing now.

But even though the Black and Latina experience is not the same, I still learned a lot because women of color can face similar challenges. Like the Latine community, the Black community is also known to assist family members financially through a "Black Tax." If you're a woman of color and the first in your family to graduate from college or earn a corporate income, you'll find we share a lot of common money struggles.

And to my white allies, thank you for being here and for your willingness to learn. If your whiteness is slightly offended while reading this book, then I've done my job well. Because I didn't write it for the white gaze. I hope you can push through that discomfort and learn what First Gen and other marginalized communities are up against in their money journeys. Use this information to be a better ally. And if this isn't your jam, I know of fifty other money books I can point you to.

How This Book Is Organized

Now that we've covered some of the reasons why this book is needed in our First Gen community let's talk about the layout of the content and what you can expect to learn.

In Chapter 1, "A Different Starting Line," we'll uncover how the First Gen money experience is different from that of most Americans. Being the first in my family to graduate from college gave me a false sense of security. I mistakenly thought that because I had earned a Bachelor's, I'd be on a level playing field with others.

Although having a college degree did open doors that my family never had access to, I learned I had a different starting line than others in the race toward financial prosperity. Had I known these differences were at play, I would have been much more proactive with my money journey sooner. I'm hoping that chapter will do the same for you. We'll compare these differences and how privilege and having immigrant roots play a role by following the money journey of three characters: Privileged Patty, Average Amy, and First Gen Gina.

In Chapter 2, "How Our Cultura Affects Our Money Experience," you'll read about the systemic barriers, cultural differences, money mindsets, and immigrant money habits that can be hurdles in your financial journey. You'll also learn how our cultura and family shape how we interact with finances, and the two-step method I use to set financial boundaries. Now I'm going to be honest:

Chapter 2 may be hard for you to get through. It was hard for me to write. There is no existing money book that tackles these taboo themes as I do.

But I know firsthand how powerful it can be to become more aware and bring light to some of the limiting money beliefs we have in our community. If you know me from my social media content, you'll be very familiar with my "I'm just keeping it real" attitude that you know and love. I bring that same realness to that section of the book.

As you read through that chapter, I want to remind you that you are not alone. A lot of the money challenges you'll face or are currently facing are part of the collective First Gen experience, and we'll get through this together.

The first two chapters are focused on the unique barriers the First Gen community faces in their money journey. This is a key element that makes *Cultura & Cash* different from other existing money books. If you're tempted to skip these first two chapters, please don't! You'll be better prepared to tackle your finances once you have a true understanding of what we're up against.

Chapters 3 through 7 are the how-to sections of this book that cover the logistics of how money works. They're practical and actionable. Instead of jumping straight into Roth IRAs and debt-payoff strategies like most existing money books do, I'll open up each chapter with personal anecdotes of how money has positively or negatively affected my life as a young adult. Think of it as relatable money lessons with a side of *chisme*.

In one chapter, you'll learn how money kept me trapped in a toxic job that cost me my health. But in another chapter, you'll see how money gave me the confidence to leave a successful career to forge my path as an entrepreneur. How is it that money held me back in one situation but helped me thrive in another?

You see, money is neutral. It's just a tool. The same way that a knife is a tool. A knife can be used to cause physical harm to others, or it can be used to lovingly cook a nutritious meal for someone you love. The difference is how you use it.

When you can see the real impact money has had on someone else's life, money becomes relatable and important to you too. Learning how money works is suddenly not just some abstract concept you should learn when you "have more time" or "when you have a bigger salary." It's something you eagerly want to learn—not to repeat those same mistakes or something you want to master to replicate the success of others. This is why I share my great and not-so-great life experiences. With these real-life money lessons, you'll find the motivation you need to learn how to manage your finances effectively.

The First Gen Five

The content in these chapters will center around my framework, the First Gen Five. The First Gen Five include five pillars: emergency funds, budgeting, debt, credit, and investing. Don't worry! I'll break down these financial concepts into easy-to-digest terms to help you learn and feel more confident about money.

There's a lot to cover in personal finance, like home ownership, trusts and wills, insurance, crypto, and much more. All the white noise can make personal finance feel overwhelming to take in, especially when you're a beginner and didn't learn much about money at home. You may feel intimidated by all the information and decide to stick your head in the sand and avoid your finances altogether. But that's not going to help you.

This book was created to inspire action. This is why I came up with my First Gen Five. I've identified that these are the five areas that can make the most difference to First Gen just getting started in their financial journey. If you follow these teachings, you'll create a solid foundation to build on because they cover your finances from the past, in your present, and in your future. You can work on all five pillars at once, and rest assured you are taking a holistic approach to improving your finances.

A Brief Overview of Chapters 3–7

Here's a quick description of the remaining chapters:

- Chapter 3, "Emergency Funds: Your Lifeboat When Sh*t Hits the Fan," will be about building a peace of mind fund to catch you when you fall.

- Chapter 4, "Budgeting Is Your BFF," will teach you how to create a spending plan you're excited about and can actually stick to.

- Chapter 5, "Debt Should Feel Uncomfy," will show how to pay off debt to free up money to use on what's important to you.

- Chapter 6, "Credit Building: Outsmart the Credit Card Companies," will demonstrate how increasing your credit score can save you money and give you more options when you need them.

- And Chapter 7, "Investing Isn't Just for Patagonia-Vest-Wearing, Middle-Aged, White Men," will teach you the basics of how to get started investing so you don't have to work until the day you die.

At the end of each chapter, I'll also open thought-provoking conversations on how you can navigate these five areas of personal finance while managing family and cultural expectations, from how to handle loaning money to extended family to helping your younger sibling build credit to investing for your parents' retirement.

In the final chapter, I'll summarize some of the key points of *Cultura & Cash* and offer guidance on how to continue your financial journey beyond this book.

The Power of Money Affirmations

A big theme of this book is improving your money mindset. Your money mindset is your thoughts and beliefs about money. It controls the way you act, behave, and spend money which all affect your ability to meet your financial goals. To improve your finances, you have to have a positive money mindset. It's the ol' "Do you see the glass half full or half empty?" analogy. When it comes to money (and most things in life!), it's important for you to train your mind to see the glass half full. You can get access to the best money education out there, but if you don't have the right mindset, your results will fall flat.

You'll notice the beginning of every chapter starts with a money affirmation. If you already practice affirmations in your everyday life, you're in for a treat! I'll save my spiel. But if you're new to them, you may be a bit confused to see them included in a money book. What do affirmations have to do with money?

I remember when I first learned about affirmations. The side-eye was strong. They sounded so hokey. "Mhmm. So I'm supposed to say things I don't believe out loud . . . and one day they'll magically become true?" Sure, Jan.

But I promise you, they work! Science has shown us that regular practice of affirmations can change our neural pathways and can shift the way we think and feel. They may feel unnatural at first. But just like anything else, as you practice them more and more, they'll become easier and easier. DO NOT skip these! Read them out loud at the beginning of each chapter, and really sink into the feelings of what you're saying. Visualize your words, and welcome what you're stating. It's yours to claim!

The more you practice affirmations, the easier it will be to allow the good in. We can't welcome abundance into our life if we're constantly resisting it, even if it is subconsciously. With time, these affirmations will start positively affecting your money mindset.

I regularly use an affirmations app in my everyday life to help me with body positivity, personal growth, and to get more restful sleep. They do wonders for me. Don't knock them 'til you try them!

Access the *Cultura & Cash* Resource Pack

Before you continue reading, visit culturaandcash.com to download the free *Cultura & Cash* Resource Pack. I created a digital toolkit to be used alongside this book, and it's available to you for free as a reader. It's a one-stop shop with value-packed resources like a list of my favorite high-yield savings accounts to earn you the most cash, a budgeting template to easily track your income and expenses, a fillable workbook to organize and get clear on your debt, a list of my favorite brokerage firms to invest your money and start building wealth, an investing video lesson, a digital workbook to complete all the book's activities, exclusive discounts on my digital resources, and more.

Scan this QR code to gain access now.

Sign-up bonuses and interest rates change frequently, and the Cultura & Cash Resource Pack allows me to have the most up-to-date information available to you in digital format beyond the publication of this book. I've included several reminders to access the C&C Resource Pack throughout this book.

What You'll Gain After Reading This Book

Imagine what it would feel like to know you have the financial security to live life more boldly. To know that money does not control you and limit you but is a powerful tool you use to your advantage to design a life you love. What would it feel like to have the financial ability to say F U to anybody or any place that doesn't serve you? Picture a life where you have the financial means to always do what's best for you, no matter the cost.

Imagine spending your money mindfully and intuitively on what's important to you and knowing it's getting you closer to your dream lifestyle. Instead of feeling overwhelmed by your debt, you'd feel confident knowing you have a plan in place to pay it off and can almost feel the sweet, sweet feeling of the #debtfreelife. What would you do with all that disposable income now that your money isn't tied up to paying debt? Would you go to grad school or explore a career in a new industry? Would you buy a service or a product that enhances your quality of life? How would you use it toward bigger life goals or to support those you love?

In this version of you, instead of being intimidated by credit cards, you'd game the system to your benefit to help give you more flexibility when you need it most. What would it feel like to know that while you're taking care of past and current you, you're also making smart money moves to take care of future you?

How good would it feel to have the ability to help your family when they need you most while knowing your finances are thriving and on autopilot? How much easier would life be if you could clearly communicate your money values and goals to your family and set respectful boundaries where everyone knows where everything stands? Imagine how proud you'll feel when you become the go-to person in your family and friend group that can help others do better with money. The teachings of *Cultura & Cash* will help you build the financial confidence to accomplish all this and so much more!

You Can Transform Your Finances for the Better

But changing your relationship with money and improving your finances won't happen overnight. It will require a plan, commitment to that plan, and consistency. It will require a willingness to unlearn cultural teachings and break generational patterns to move differently than others in your family have. You'll have to put in work to redefine your money values. It will feel tough at times. But I know you can do it!

And how do I know? Because you've been doing hard things your whole life.

You were the first in your family to navigate FAFSA, the college application process, and make it to college. The first to navigate the maze that is academia and graduate from college when all odds were stacked against you. You beat the statistics. You may have even gone on to pursue higher education and acquired a master's or a PhD (*¡shau!*). You were the first in your family to secure a professional job in your field of study with no contacts or connections. No nepo babies here! You were the first in your family to navigate professional workspaces where nobody looks like you with little help from any mentors or sponsors.

Even as a child, you've done hard things. You served as a language interpreter for your Spanish-speaking parents at doctor appointments and parent-teacher meetings at school. You translated important mail and helped them review important legal documents. These are all hard things for grown adults to do, and you did them all as a kid!

As a First Gen, you are smart, resilient, and resourceful. Repeat this affirmation: *I can do hard things*. You've accomplished all this with a fraction of the support others have gotten, and you're *still* here. And you have me on your side as your guide to show you how you can master your money to design a life where you and those you love thrive.

CHAPTER 1

A DIFFERENT STARTING LINE

Abundance is coming. I deserve it and accept it.

A s much as social media gurus claim otherwise, nobody can truly predict when a video will go viral. Some people think you need a professionally produced, high-quality video with eye-catching effects or that you need to dress in the latest fashion trends while lip-synching to a viral song. I've spent hours working on scripting, producing, and editing a well-thought-out video, only for it to flop and get a couple hundred views. It's hit or miss.

My most viewed video was one I recorded while I was lying in bed, ready to wind down and call it a night. Like any good TikTok junkie, I was up late mindlessly scrolling when I got the idea for a video. It took me less than five minutes to put together, and within days it got 4.4 million views, 1.1 million likes, and over 35,000 comments. For weeks, my cell phone buzzed nonstop with new notification updates. The video had gone mega-viral!

Looking back, I know why the video evoked a strong reaction from the internet. I'd reposted a controversial cartoon and added the caption, "For my black and brown sisters #keepfighting #POC #BIPOC."

The reposted cartoon depicts two people at the starting line of a track and field race—a cocky white man smiling in a suit in one lane and a Black woman with a determined scowl in athletic clothes in the other lane. It's clear that her lane looks drastically different from his. His lane has a couple of undersized hurdles pushed off to the side. Her lane is crowded with obstacles— barbed wire, a crocodile pit, a crumbling brick wall, and sharp spears shooting up from the ground. She's wearing a heavy ball and chain on her ankle that's already weighing her down before she even starts the race. The cartoon's caption, spoken by the man, says: "What's the matter? It's the same distance!" To drive the point home, I added an audio that said, "It's not fair, it's not fair," over and over as the background sound to the video.

As you can imagine, the comments section was a dumpster fire with users chiming in with their opposing opinions. Some people argued women of color are given more opportunities than white men nowadays. The kinder comments supported the message. But my favorite comment said: "And she still wins."

A Different Starting Line

Similar to the cartoon where women of color face unfair obstacles in their careers, First Gen face many challenges on their road to financial freedom. Not only do we encounter challenges others don't, I'd argue that our starting line is different and further back than those of our peers. Which means we have some catching up to do. To understand our starting point and the work that lies ahead, I think it's important to compare and contrast the financial journeys of some of our peers.

Let's go back to our race example. In the race to financial freedom, we have three types of racers: Privileged Patty, Average Amy, and First Gen Gina. All three characters come from different walks of life. What sets them apart the most from each other is their level of privilege, which is mostly tied to their family's immigration history. We'll get a glimpse of how privilege and their proximity to the immigrant experience affect their money journey at different phases of their life. We'll compare and contrast each character's experience beginning from their childhood through young adulthood.

Keep this in mind: As you read through the comparisons, a lot of it will sound unrelatable and may even turn you off. It may feel uncomfortable to learn about what others had when you didn't have the same opportunities. You may be tempted to put the book down or to skip ahead. Stick with me here. It's by design. These three characters and their experiences were thoughtfully included in this book for a reason. At the end of the chapter, you'll understand why we had to expose these differences. Instead of getting discouraged, use this knowledge and the teachings in this book to fuel your journey toward financial freedom.

Privileged Patty

LIFE AS A CHILD:

Privileged Patty is a fifth-generation American. Her ancestors were immigrants and moved their family to America five generations ago. Her family is well entrenched in the US financial system, which they used to their benefit to freely build wealth for themselves and future generations.

Growing up, Privileged Patty had two loving, financially literate parents who held regular and transparent money discussions with her. Financial education had been passed down by the previous generations, so her parents had witnessed firsthand how financial literacy could enrich their lives and the lives of future generations. Now they wanted to pass on those teachings to their daughter so she, too, could be financially successful.

At age ten, they sat her down and explained how they balanced their checkbook every month to pay the household bills. They gave her a weekly allowance for doing her household chores on time, like cleaning her bedroom or walking the family dog. They taught her it was unwise to spend her allowance all in one place and instead encouraged her to save a portion of it for the future. They incentivized her to save by offering to match her savings. For every $100 she added to her savings, they'd add another $100 of their own money, essentially doubling her savings rate. This motivated Privileged Patty to get into the habit of saving money at a young age.

As she went on to her teenage years, they started teaching her more complex topics, like the importance of using credit cards responsibly to build a good credit score, why she should avoid debt, and why investing in the stock market was important to her financial future. They drove her to their local bank to open her first checking and savings account and explained to her how the accounts worked. They added her to their credit line as an authorized user, so she got to benefit from building credit while only being a teenager. The early exposure to money management as a child helped her successfully navigate finances as a young adult. Instead of feeling scared of money, she felt confident and excited about her financial future.

Average Amy

LIFE AS A CHILD:

Average Amy is a second-generation American. Her grandparents were immigrants and moved their family to America for the opportunity to live a better life. Her parents weren't experts in the US financial system but had learned a thing or two about finances in the few decades their family lived in the States.

Growing up, Average Amy had two loving, somewhat financially literate parents who taught her basic money principles. Amy's parents grew up hearing stories about the financial hardships their parents experienced as new immigrants in America. They didn't want their child to struggle like past generations had, so they did their best to teach Average Amy the value of a dollar.

Her family didn't talk as openly about money as Privileged Patty's family did. They had limited financial knowledge on more complicated topics, like investing and credit building, so they couldn't share much on those subjects. They had a better understanding of the benefits of saving and avoiding debt, so they always encouraged Average Amy to be responsible and save her allowance.

Average Amy received a small monthly allowance from her parents for doing household chores. One weekday afternoon, her mom watched an episode of *Oprah* where a financial expert explained the benefits of teaching children how to budget. Average Amy's mom was very inspired by the TV episode and decided to teach her twelve-year-old daughter how to use a budget with her allowance money to help pay for her cheerleading summer camp. This helped her see in real time how saving and budgeting could help her pay for things she enjoyed. It made saving fun because she loved cheerleading camp with her friends!

When Average Amy turned sixteen, she got a part-time job working at a nearby movie theater. This was her first time earning money outside of her allowance, and she was excited to have the freedom to buy the clothes and shoes she wanted. No more begging her parents for extra spending money! Her parents drove her to their bank to open her first checking account and explained how her direct deposit worked. The bank clerk asked her parents if they were interested in applying for a credit card while they were there. They politely declined and warned Average Amy that to avoid credit card debt, she should avoid credit cards altogether.

First Gen Gina

LIFE AS A CHILD:

First Gen Gina is a first-generation American. When her parents were in their twenties, they left everything they knew, their family, friends, culture, and language in México, to move to America. They moved to the US with no connections and little savings but big hopes to give their future children a better life in their new country.

First Gen Gina grew up in a loving, hardworking, low-income, immigrant household. During the day, her dad worked in construction and, during the evening, at a local car wash. Her mom worked long ten-hour shifts as a seamstress. Their jobs didn't pay very well, so they worked tirelessly around the clock to keep a roof over their head, clothes on their back, and food on their table.

The family didn't have much, but they knew they were better off than their family back in México and often reminded their children of that. They were grateful they had the opportunity to emigrate to the US and cover their family's basic needs with honest and hard work. First Gen Gina and her younger siblings were often told that if they worked hard and went to college, they could have a good life.

Money wasn't ever discussed at home. Since her parents were new immigrants to the country, they had limited knowledge of the US financial system. Plus, after paying rent, groceries, and all other bills for a family of five, there was little money left over at the end of the month. Their biggest priority was surviving in a new country and keeping the lights on. They already had a full plate of tasks: learning a new language, being far away from their extended family, and adopting a new way of life—the American way. In their eyes, paying the bills on time was a win in itself.

Although money wasn't discussed, she could sense there wasn't enough of it. When she was a child, she enjoyed flipping through the Scholastic book fair catalog. There were so many things she could buy, like colorful gel pens or big, wacky stickers she could use to decorate her lunchbox. She smiled at the possibilities. She was a big fan of the *Goosebumps* series and really wanted to ask her parents for some money to buy a book at the fair. But she had overheard her parents talking about how her dad's hours at the car wash had been cut and money being tight for the month. She didn't want to make it harder for her parents by asking for money. After that, First Gen Gina learned not to ask for money, but she still enjoyed skimming over the books at the book fair every time it was in town.

When First Gen Gina turned sixteen, she got a part-time job working at an ice cream shop. She'd never received an allowance for doing the household chores, so this was the first time she had her own money. She was so excited! Her parents were proud to see their oldest daughter grow up to be a responsible and hardworking young adult. They encouraged her to do well at her new job but reminded her that her education and going to college should be her top priority. They didn't want to see her struggle with a minimum-wage job like they did. They reminded her that the reason they left México was to give her and her brothers a better life, and that included seeing them go to college.

When she got her first check from the ice cream shop, her mom took her to their bank to open a checking account. Nobody at the bank spoke Spanish, so First Gen Gina helped translate and read the legal forms to her mom. Her mom told her she was proud she was earning her own money but warned her not to spend it all. "Don't make the mistakes we made. We haven't saved a lot of money. Put some money aside in case you need it."

Privileged Patty
LIFE DURING COLLEGE:

During college, Privileged Patty's parents covered 100 percent of her college expenses. Thanks to their financial adviser, they'd been planning for their daughter's college education since she was an infant, and they had the financial means to pay large expenses like her tuition, books, and housing. They also gave her a monthly allowance to cover other living expenses, like groceries and social outings with her new university friends. Her parents paid for her phone bill and health insurance throughout school. If she wanted to pick up a part-time job to earn some extra cash, she could, but she was at ease knowing her basic living expenses were fully met. Her only responsibility as a student was to get good grades and not overspend her monthly allowance.

This financial privilege allowed her to attend and graduate from college debt free. Like any new college student, she had her share of challenges: She was adjusting to a new environment, meeting new friends, and juggling a full course load, but fortunately for her, money was never a worry. She knew her parents were only a phone call away and could always help if a financial emergency came up. If she overspent her allowance, they could readily transfer more money to her account—with a slap on the wrist, of course! This made her college experience less stressful and allowed her to immerse herself in student life and the college experience fully.

Average Amy
LIFE DURING COLLEGE:

Before attending college, Average Amy's parents had a difficult conversation with her. They told her they opened a college savings account when she was born but didn't start making serious contributions until she was ten years old. This meant her college choices were a bit limited. They explained they only had enough money to cover her school expenses if she attended a public state university. If she wanted to attend a private or out-of-state university, she could, but she'd have to pay for it out of her own pocket—and take on debt.

Average Amy felt frustrated. A lot of her friends were going to more prestigious out-of-state schools, and she wanted to experience the same. But she understood that having her parents help with tuition, room and board, and books at a public state university could help her avoid student debt. Since her parents had warned her of the dangers of debt as a child, she decided to go to a public state university to avoid taking on student loans. Another added benefit is that they also kept her on their family's health insurance plan, which saved her a great deal of money since she wasn't required to buy the university's mandatory health insurance plan.

She was expected to get a part-time job to cover her living expenses like groceries and entertainment money. She found a part-time job as a server at a restaurant downtown, which was about a thirty-minute car ride from her dorm room. The distance was too far for her to bike there, and public transportation wasn't reliable, so she found herself in need of a car. Luckily, her grandma was looking to sell her used vehicle. She agreed to sell her a well-maintained, low-mileage 2010 Toyota Camry for $5,000, which was well below the going rate for that type of car. Average Amy used her cash savings from her teenage working years to buy the car from her grandmother. The timing couldn't have been better! Had it not been for Grandma selling her a car at a discounted rate, she would have had to use more of her hard-earned savings to buy a different car. Or, even worse, need a car loan from a used car lot and get herself into debt.

Average Amy had a harder time adjusting to her new college schedule. Although her part-time job was only twelve hours a week, it still took a lot of planning and organizing to make sure she had enough time for her full coursework, assignments, job, and social life. When finals season came around, she vented to her parents that she was feeling overwhelmed with her packed schedule. Her parents suggested she cut back her hours at work and reassured her they'd cover her groceries and other living expenses while she was preparing for finals. Average Amy took full advantage of their offer, promptly notified her boss, and used the extra time available to prepare for her exams. She crushed finals season with As and Bs.

With her parents' financial support, she graduated from college with a strong GPA and only $15,000 in student debt. Having her parent's financial backing during this time was invaluable. Although she had a busy college life, her stress never resulted from money. Her parents were only a phone call away, and if she were ever in a serious financial pickle, they'd find a way to (begrudgingly) provide support to their daughter.

First Gen Gina
LIFE DURING COLLEGE:

When First Gen Gina was a senior in high school, she started applying for college. She wasn't sure what college would be the best fit for her. Her parents hadn't attended college, so they couldn't give her much guidance, which meant she had to learn how to fill out the applications and FAFSA all on her own. Her family didn't have the financial means or work flexibility to drive her to tour different university campuses, so she did most of her research by watching YouTube videos online. Who needs campus tours when you have the internet?

She was so happy when she got accepted into the university of her choice. A lot of her high school friends were going to college there too. She was going to be the first in her family to attend college! Her parents beamed with pride. While she was excited to start a new chapter, she also felt a little guilty for leaving her family and being away from them.

Soon after getting accepted, she got the financial aid award letter.

Financial aid would cover a lot of her college expenses (phew!), but she still had an outstanding balance of $20,000 for the first year to cover tuition and room and board. Her parents didn't have health insurance, which meant she'd also have to sign up for the mandatory health insurance plan, which added another couple hundred dollars to her tuition bill.

Although her parents were very supportive of her getting a higher education, they told her they didn't have the money to help pay for it. Money was already tight around the house as it was, especially since they were sending a small allowance to Gina's grandma back in México. This meant First Gen Gina was on her own for all college expenses, including her living expenses like groceries, phone bills, and outings with friends.

The award letter had some helpful information on student loans. Subsidized and unsubsidized federal student loans could help cover the gap. She didn't know what subsidized and unsubsidized meant. All she knew was that she needed to go to college and needed money to pay for it.

She understood the importance of a degree for her and her family's future. She didn't want to struggle with money as her parents had, and she knew a college education was a sure way to help her earn a higher income. She figured that once she graduated from college, she'd be making more money and would have no problem paying the loans back. She didn't want to be another statistic—another Latina college dropout. She had to graduate no matter what, and money couldn't stand in her way. Besides, one of her high school teachers had once told her student debt was "good debt." She signed on for the maximum amount of loans available to her and started school that fall semester.

Campus life was a bit chaotic. She had a full course load and a part-time job as a barista at a coffee shop on campus. Adjusting to campus life was hard. She wasn't sure she was taking the right classes to graduate on time and wasn't getting the best grades, even though she was studying harder than she'd ever had. She didn't have any older siblings or even cousins who could teach her the ropes of college life, and whenever she vented to her parents about some of her new struggles, the only words of encouragement they could offer were a cheerful "Tu échale ganas, mija."

It was a constant juggling act to balance school, work, and friendships, and she wasn't very good at it. When things got hectic during midterms and finals season, she often fantasized about quitting her barista job. She knew that if she worked less and had more time and energy to study, she'd get better grades. But quitting wasn't an option. She needed the money for basic living expenses like to pay her groceries and phone bill. She was also using the money she earned at her part-time job to help her parents back home.

Since moving away for college, her dad's hours at work had been cut again, so she started paying their electricity bill to help them out. Even though she didn't have much herself and she was barely scraping by on her $15/hour barista job, she felt a responsibility to them as the oldest daughter and the one who'd made it to college. Her parents had sacrificed so much for her and her siblings by immigrating to the US, and the least she could do was help them when they needed her.

She quickly dismissed the idea of quitting school and toughed it out. It was stressful to balance it all, her mental health and her grades suffered, but at least she knew she was a good daughter to her hardworking parents.

Privileged Patty
LIFE POST-COLLEGE:

Privileged Patty graduated completely debt free. Since she had her parents' full financial support, she never had to borrow student debt.

Luckily, she was also able to stay clear of credit card debt too, since she'd been warned of the dangers of it at such a young age.

Her parents were a tremendous help during her post-graduation job search. They had professional jobs themselves, so they helped her create a résumé, taught her how to write a cover letter, and practiced answering common interview questions. They even had some contacts in their network who could open doors at some desirable corporations for Privileged Patty to interview with.

Once she was offered a job, her parents taught her how to advocate for herself and negotiate her salary, which helped her increase her starting pay by 10 percent. When she was onboarding as a new employee, they helped her sift through her new employee packets and explained the workplace benefits her new job offered, which included health insurance, life insurance, and retirement accounts. With their guidance, she signed up for the health insurance plan that carried the deductible and copay that made the most financial sense for her. Patty's parents encouraged her to opt into her workplace retirement plan to start investing for retirement. They explained how the elusive company match worked and advised her to contribute at least up to the match as it's considered "free money." With their guidance, she was able to take full advantage of the workplace benefits at her new firm.

Privileged Patty's parents understood that life as a new adult could be challenging on an entry-level salary, so they agreed to gift her a monthly allowance of $300 for her first year as a working professional to help make the transition smoother. They also paid the deposit for her new apartment in the city, which helped her live in a desirable neighborhood a short drive from the office. As a graduation gift, they gifted her a lightly used vehicle to commute to her new job.

Like any young adult, Privileged Patty was nervous about starting her first big-girl job. There was a lot to learn in her new role, but she always knew she could lean on her parents for additional support, whether it was financial or professional advice.

Average Amy
LIFE POST-COLLEGE:

Average Amy graduated from college and entered adulthood with a relatively small amount—$15,000—in student debt. Although she'd learned from her parents that carrying debt could negatively affect her finances, she wasn't too worried about the $15,000. She was sure that with her new corporate salary, she could easily pay off the balance in a few years.

Her parents were a great help during her job search. Although they didn't have an extensive network, they, too, were working professionals. They knew the basics of interviewing and writing résumés, so they helped her work on her résumé and practice reciting her interview answers.

Once she started her job, they sat down with her and helped her elect benefits, which included a 401(k) and a company match. Although they didn't know much about the ins and outs of investing, they encouraged her to opt into the company retirement plan and secure the employer match. They hadn't taken advantage of their own retirement investing until midway through their careers and didn't want their daughter to make the same mistake.

Her benefits package also included health insurance, dental, and vision. While reviewing her benefits, Average Amy noticed her employer's health insurance premiums were quite hefty—$400 a month. She panicked. Should she decline the coverage? There's no way she could afford that! But she needs health insurance.

Fortunately, it only cost $100 for her to stay on her parent's family plan, and they were willing to let her stay in it until she aged out at twenty-six. After that, she'd have to find her own health insurance. She was relieved. Because she has access to her parent's plan, she'd have affordable insurance for the next five years. She figured once she was twenty-six, she'd be at a different employer anyway. For now, she had an extra $300 in savings to use toward her financial goals, like paying off her student debt or building her savings, instead of throwing money down the drain on an overpriced insurance premium.

Average Amy's parents recognized their daughter still needed financial support as she transitioned from college graduate to working adult. To help with costs, they suggested she move back home with them, rent-free, for the next two years. At first, Average Amy complained, wanting to keep her independence. But after some discussions, they convinced her that saving on rent costs would help her pay off her student debt more quickly. Since she wouldn't pay for housing, she'd also have the ability to build her savings account and maybe even start a down payment fund for her first home.

It wasn't fun to be a mid-twenty-year-old living at her parents' house. Like anyone that age, she wanted her own space. But the sacrifice was well worth it. Years later, Average Amy would look back at this time and name it one of the best financial decisions she ever made.

First Gen Gina
LIFE POST-COLLEGE:

Graduation day finally came! She was so proud of herself for being the first in her family to graduate from a four-year university and to set a good example for her siblings. They, too, could go to college one day, and now they'd have someone who could show them the ropes!

First Gen Gina entered adulthood with $80,000 in student loans and no job prospects. Unlike Privileged Patty and Average

Amy, she had no connections in corporate America who could help her land a job or point her in the right direction, so she started her job search with no leads. This made the process drawn out and a lot more stressful because she knew she had to start making payments on her student debt soon.

After months of stumbling through résumé writing and interview prepping all on her own, she finally got a job offer. The recruiter offered her a starting role for $45,000. She didn't know negotiating was even an option, so she accepted the job offer on the spot. After all, $45,000 was more than either of her parents had ever earned in their jobs, and she was just thankful to land an offer after months and months of searching.

While filling out the onboarding paperwork, she came across her benefits package and felt overwhelmed by all the options and intimidating jargon. PPO, HMO, and 401 ¿que? What did all these things mean? And did she really need them? She asked the HR lady—an unfriendly chain smoker—for guidance, but she wasn't much help. She couldn't turn to her parents because they'd never had a job that offered them these types of benefits. Just like in college, she was left on her own to figure it out.

While sifting through her paperwork, she learned the 401(k) plan was a retirement plan for company employees. She was only twenty-three—did she really need to start thinking about retirement now? She was young and just starting out her career. Retirement seemed so far away. She decided to skip it for now. She told herself she'd revisit it later when she was further along in her career and making more money. First, she had to determine whether her new salary would even be enough to cover her new lifestyle as a working professional.

She didn't have any financial support from her parents—if anything, she was expected to help her family with additional expenses now that she had a full-time job. She was completely on her own to pay for her rent and all her living expenses, in addition to almost six figures in student debt to worry about. A little part of her squirmed inside since she wasn't entirely sure how she'd pay off $80,000 in debt, but she quickly brushed the thought off.

As for housing, she thought about moving back home like her other classmates, but there really wasn't much space in her childhood home now. Her brothers were older now and couldn't share rooms anymore. Living at home wasn't an option. She searched for her own apartment and found a unit a short twenty-minute drive to her new office.

It was a small studio apartment, but it was clean, came with a parking spot, and was in the safe part of town. She needed money for the deposit before moving in. Her parents couldn't help, and the little savings she had from her barista job were long gone. Luckily one of her close college friends was able to loan her the deposit, and she was able to move in.

A few months into her new job, life was good! She was making more money than she'd ever had and was able to make the minimum payments on her student debt. With her stable salary, she now had money to spend on things she always wanted, like shopping trips and nice dinners out with friends. She'd applied for a credit card earlier in the year and was approved. She used it frequently when out with friends. She didn't know much about credit cards, but she knew other friends had them and felt she should too.

Before she knew it, these outings started to add up. She checked her credit card balance, and she now owed $5,000 in credit card debt. The odd thing was that even though she paid the minimum payment every month, the balance didn't change much. It didn't make sense, but she promised herself she'd do better next month.

Privileged Patty

CULTURAL EXPECTATIONS AT PLAY:

As a fifth-generation American, Privileged Patty is not expected to support her family financially. Her parents have their finances all in order, which includes stable housing, health insurance, healthy savings, and a growing retirement account. When she goes out to dinner with family, she can't even pay the restaurant tab as a thank you! The unspoken rule was that her parents would always pay.

Instead of giving money to family, Privileged Patty's parents continued to support her through other young adult milestones financially. When she got engaged, her parents surprised her by sharing that they had $30,000 set aside to help cover a large portion of her wedding expenses. As she grew in her career and started considering home ownership, her parents loaned her the money for her down payment—interest-free and with flexible payments. When Privileged Patty's dear old Grandma Gertrude passed away, she inherited $50,000. She planned to use the money to attend graduate school or to remodel her home, she wasn't sure yet, but at least she had options.

With this continued financial support, Privileged Patty was able to focus solely on building wealth for herself and her future children.

Must be nice, huh? Privileged Patty was set up for success. Sure, she did her part by graduating from college and putting in the work at her full-time job, but it's hard to fail when a lot of barriers are cleared out for you. You get a piggyback ride to the front of the finish line and have a safety net to catch you when you fall. The generational wealth and generational knowledge she received from her family made it much easier to succeed. The odds were in her favor from the start.

Average Amy
CULTURAL EXPECTATIONS AT PLAY:

As a second-generation American, Average Amy was not expected to support her family financially. Although her parents weren't exactly knocking back champagne on a yacht with Jeff Bezos, they were financially secure in their own right. They didn't have all money matters figured out, but they had some savings they could tap into and investments of their own. If they ever came across a financial emergency, like suddenly needing a new HVAC system or money for an unexpected medical expense, their adult children would be the last people they'd ask for help.

Instead, Average Amy's parents continued to provide financial support, but in a much smaller capacity. When she turned thirty, her parents gifted her $10,000 to use toward her down payment fund. The unexpected gift helped Average Amy feel supported and less stressed about her finances and helped her continue to dodge debt. Because of their continued support, she achieved home ownership and started building equity at the age of thirty-two.

A couple of years later, when it was time to sell her new home, her parents loaned her $10,000 to help remodel it first. She saved money by rolling up her sleeves and doing some of the work herself. With the remodel, her home's value increased, and she was able to sell the property for an additional $50,000. That gave her a nice boost in her net worth!

When Average Amy's dear old Grandma Agnes passed away, she received a small inheritance of $20,000. By that time, she was paying her way through grad school, so she used all the inheritance money toward tuition and avoided an additional $20,000 in student loans.

With this continued financial support, Average Amy was able to focus solely on building wealth for herself and her future children.

She felt at ease knowing her aging parents had a nest egg of their own. It felt reassuring to know that when retirement came around for them, they'd be okay.

I've noticed an interesting pattern with the Average Amys in my life. They usually only credit their hard work for their success and not the privilege and generational knowledge they inherited from their family.

"But I've worked for everything I've had!" and "My parents didn't give me anything!" is what I usually hear from these close friends when I challenge their privilege.

And it's true. Average Amys didn't get to benefit from the same level of privilege and access as Privileged Pattys. Average Amys had to put in their share of work. They were smart enough to take advantage of the resources and support their parents provided to them, and they worked hard to do their part.

But they didn't always make the best choices; they were *given* the best choices. And that's still a level of privilege that's worth acknowledging.

First Gen Gina
CULTURAL EXPECTATIONS AT PLAY:

As a first-generation American, First Gen Gina was expected to support her family financially. Her parents were still living off a low income, and they welcomed all the help they could get from their oldest daughter. They had no savings of their own and lived paycheck to paycheck. In her family's culture, it was very normal to lean on relatives whenever money issues came up, no matter the cost. It's what's expected when it comes to family.

While Privileged Patty and Average Amy had financial support through adult milestones, First Gen Gina had to fund large purchases, like making a down payment on a home, paying for a wedding, or covering the costs of grad school all on her own. When her Abuelita Mariela passed away later that year, instead of receiving an inheritance, she was forwarded a bill to help cover the burial costs. No generational wealth here.

Some onlookers may see this and think: "This poor young woman. Instead of focusing on herself and creating a life of her own, she's always burdened with family responsibilities." But First Gen Gina doesn't feel burdened by family—she feels honored she gets to help her family and be there for them when they most need it.

But she does worry whether it will be enough. Not only does she have to support herself, but she also has to consider her aging parents and think about how she can help them retire. Her dad's body is already breaking down on him—he can't work his construction job forever. She knows her parents don't have any retirement savings. Will she earn enough to support herself and her parents pay off her debt, and build toward the future? She's thankful she's in a position where she can think about helping others, but sometimes the responsibility can feel overwhelming and heavy.

Does any of this sound painfully familiar? If it does, don't worry. I got you. You're in the right place.

Did you spot the difference in money experiences?

Now, what was the point of me walking you through the distinct money journeys of these three characters? Do I get joy out of pointing out what we don't have? Of course not! After reading the three different life experiences, you should have noticed some patterns.

Privileged Patty got a big head start in life when her family taught her how to manage her money at such a young age. The generational knowledge she inherited helped her make smarter money choices as a teenager and young adult, like dodging debt and prioritizing investing. She also got to benefit from generational wealth through major life transitions in early adulthood, helping her avoid debt and creating more space to plan for her financial future. Privileged Patty could have been stressed about many things in life, but money was never one of them. According to a survey conducted by the Federal Reserve, the top 10 percent of wealthiest Americans received an average inheritance of $174,200 (excluding the one-percenters).[1]

Although Average Amy did not receive the same level of financial support that Privileged Patty did, the generational knowledge she gained still helped tremendously and gave her a big advantage as a young adult. Even though she didn't learn the intricacies of the stock market as Privileged Patty did, she did gain some financial basics. And some knowledge is better than no knowledge. It helped her minimize her debt burden, which freed up her money to focus on her own financial goals. With her family's early teaching on budgeting, she responsibly managed the money she earned at her job. Her financial journey was a much smoother ride. According to the Federal Reserve, 40 percent of households receive an average inheritance of $45,900.

Another thing both characters have in common is they have the luxury of just focusing on their own finances and nothing else. Any money they earned was solely for them and future generations. They didn't have the additional responsibility of providing for their parents or extended family. The majority of the Latine

1   Reed, Eric. "Average American Inheritance, By Wealth Level." Yahoo! Finance, July 7, 2023. https://finance.yahoo.com/news/average-american-inheritance-wealth-level-130120356.html?guccounter=1#:~:text=Bottom%20Line,those%20in%20the%20bottom%20half.

community does not have this same advantage. According to a Bank of America study, 72 percent of Latine Millennials provide financial support to family, which disproportionally affects our ability to build financial security.[2]

The Privilege Is Real

Do you think my illustration of privilege sounded exaggerated? It's not. All these stories are real. Although the characters I created are fictitious, the anecdotes are all true stories. To write this book, I surveyed some of my friends and former colleagues, all with varying levels of privilege, to gather stories of how money management was taught in their homes or how their families provided them with financial support through different adult milestones.

I don't point these differences out to vilify anyone. Privileged Patty and Average Amy are not bad people for having had an easier path than us (although I wish more of them acknowledged and credited the privilege that helped them succeed in life more often instead of just chalking it up to "hard work"—but I digress). Good for them! And good job to the parents for setting them up for success. It's what any loving parent who has the *ability* would do.

We May Not Have the Privilege, But We Do Have the Ambition

The goal of this book is to teach you how to master money management so that you can be the catalyst for creating Privileged Patricias and Average Almas in your life.

---

2   "More Than 70 percent of Hispanic Millennials Providing Financial Support to Family Members—With Many Increasing Their Support During the Pandemic," Businesswire, August 18, 2021.

Because the truth is there will always be someone who has more than you. It's the reality of the society we live in. There will always be someone smarter, richer, and better connected than you.

But the reason I compared and contrasted the different levels of privilege is because, to me, it was pretty eye-opening to understand that it's not just the one-percenters who grow up privileged and get to benefit from their family's success. The average middle-class American *also* has a much easier path, just from having had their family immigrate to this country a couple of generations ago and having college-educated parents who can show them the ropes.

Financial success is more attainable for families who no longer bear the weight of immigrant struggles. The further a family is from the immigrant experience—the easier it is for them to build wealth in this country.

If a family immigrated to this country generations ago, they *should* have achieved a college education and encouraged their kids to follow their path. They *should* have somewhat of an understanding of the financial system and pass this information on to their loved ones. They *should* have some level of generational wealth and be able to pass on money to their children.

As First-Gen, we lack this generational knowledge and generational wealth. In fact, only 7 percent of Latine households reported receiving an inheritance, versus almost 30 percent of white American households.[3] We don't get the blueprint for financial success. We have to learn it all on our own and teach our family along the way. The limited support can affect our mental health and our

---

3   Bhutta, Neil, Andrew C. Chang, Lisa J. Dettling, and Joanne W. Hsu, "Disparities in Wealth by Race and Ethnicity in the 2019 Survey of Consumer Finances," FEDS Notes, September 28, 2020, https://www.federalreserve.gov/econres/notes/feds-notes/disparities-in-wealth-by-race-and-ethnicity-in-the-2019-survey-of-consumer-finances-20200928.html.

ability to build wealth. When we have more debt, less financial support, and more financial responsibilities to our extended family, it's more challenging to save and plan for our own future.

To Do Better, We Must Know Better

My goal in sharing these three different experiences is to illustrate that the challenges of being First Gen span well past our college graduation. We do not have the same starting point.

I know firsthand that it can feel like a lonely and uphill battle when you lack financial guidance, start life in the negative, and have family obligations to meet. But as the first in your family to be in new spaces, you are resilient, gritty, and resourceful. You wouldn't have accomplished all that you had if you weren't. Because it damn sure wasn't privilege that got you here!

Building financial security and generational wealth is possible for you too. I wouldn't have bothered writing this book if I didn't believe that to my core. But since our starting line is different, it will require more work and intentionality. You'll have to unlearn limiting money beliefs you inherited from your family and culture. You'll need to be the first in your family to break generational patterns and do things differently. It won't happen on its own. You'll need awareness and a plan. And to create a plan, you'll need to understand how money works and what cultural norms are holding you back.

This is where I come in!

THE FIRST GEN FIVE WILL GUIDE YOU

The majority of this book will focus on my First Gen Five framework to help you close this gap and catch up. If you focus on the top five money pillars, you'll be on your way to creating a solid money foundation for yourself, your family, and future generations to come. Those five pillars are as follows:

- Building a peace of mind fund to protect you when you need it
- Creating a spending plan you can actually stick to
- Eliminating debt to create more space to fund your life goals
- Hacking your credit score to give you flexibility and options
- Learning the basics of investing to build long-term wealth and achieve financial freedom

But before we get there, we first need to tackle some cultural barriers that can be an obstacle to our financial journey. In Chapter 2, you'll learn why your parents may be resistant to making different money choices and how it can affect the way you interact with money. It may be hard to read. It emphasizes the importance of breaking generational patterns—deciding to do things differently than your family can make you feel like you're betraying your family and your culture. It's an important chapter which is why I've included it in this book.

If Chapter 2 starts feeling heavy, feel free to read it in smaller doses. Take the time you need but see it through to the end. The worst thing you can do is close the book and not finish it. At the very minimum, move forward to Chapter 3 and beyond, where I share the more practical money tips you can use to set yourself up for financial success. You can always go back and read that section when you're ready.

The Beginning of a Brighter Financial Future

As we wrap up this chapter, I want to share this. If you feel a little discouraged after reading all the support others got along the way, that's okay. It's normal to feel that way. If you feel behind, it's for a reason. The reality is we are not starting at the same starting line.

But instead of letting it stunt you, use it as a wake-up call to be proactive and take charge of your money. Use this as the motivation you need to learn, put in the work, and catch up. And think about this: By choosing to be intentional with your money now, you can be that person who forever changes the financial trajectory of your family and helps future generations thrive. The same way that your immigrant parents were the brave change-makers who left everything behind to give you and generations to come the opportunity to achieve more. You *can* do this because you have all that you need within you to transform your finances for the better.

CHAPTER 2

HOW OUR CULTURA
AFFECTS OUR
MONEY EXPERIENCE

I am on the path to becoming the first millionaire in my family.

"**Y**our speaker application has been accepted!" read the email headline on my iPhone screen. Could my eyes be playing tricks on me? My heart rate thumped like a drum, and my mind raced as I reread the headline in disbelief. I held my breath, and my eyes hopped around the phone screen as I speed-read the rest of the email. I'd been selected to be a speaker at FinCon 2021!

FinCon is a huge financial convention for money content creators like your favorite YouTubers, authors, bloggers, podcasters, influencers . . . and yes, TikTokers. Comic book nerds go to Comic-Con, money nerds go to FinCon. Anybody who's anybody in the personal finance world attends FinCon.

I had submitted a speaker application as a delusional baddie but never thought I'd actually get accepted. After all, I'd only been a content creator for four months. Some of these people had been at it for years—or decades! As a personal finance lover, I'd been following the convention for a while, and now I had an opportunity not just to attend but to speak alongside financial experts whom I'd admired and followed for ages. This was the real deal!

I was excited to speak at the convention and to establish myself as a leader in the personal finance arena. I had quit my corporate job in investment management only a couple of months before. I knew that speaking at FinCon was a good opportunity to shed my corporate identity and transition fully to my new career as a financial educator. This is just what I needed!

But, like anybody doing something new for the first time, my mind started racing with negative self-talk of all the things that could go wrong.

What if I forget my speech halfway through and have a one-sided staring contest with the audience? What if I ramble and say a whole lot of nothing and go over my allotted thirty minutes? What if nobody attends my session, and I have to speak to an empty room? Or even worse, what if people *do attend* but find me boring AF and leave halfway through my presentation? ¡Que vergüenza!

Out of all the nerve-racking scenarios I played out in my head, the one I never considered was the one that actually happened: ugly crying on stage. Like mocos running down my nose and desperately gasping for air type of ugly crying. You know, that kind.

Who knew a speech about budgeting or Roth IRAs could be that deep, right?

But my presentation was anything but light and vanilla. The topic I presented was called "Wealth Building as a First-Generation American." In the presentation, I talked about some of the cultural and systemic barriers First Gen face in our financial journey. The conversation was raw and real. I drew from my lived experience and shared personal anecdotes of the difficult times I'd had navigating money with my family. It wasn't easy, but I managed to keep it together and get through my thirty minutes without showing any signs of emotion.

But during the Q and A portion, a woman in the audience raised one hand and tearfully said with a tissue in the other, "Nobody ever talks about these issues and how they affect our community. It can feel really lonely to go through all of this on our own. Thank you for talking about this." I suddenly felt all the feels. My vulnerability and storytelling had helped a fellow Latina feel seen, understood, and less alone. Her tearful reaction disarmed the brave face I had put on. I started empathizing and crying with her when an audience member approached me on stage to hand me a tissue too. A few other audience attendees joined us in crying.

While others may have felt unprofessional or like a failure for crying on stage, I now look back at that moment and feel proud of my vulnerability and willingness to take on such heavy topics. It moved my audience so much that we formed a real connection and stayed long after my presentation to swap similar stories with one another. We were in community.

Those complex topics are what this chapter is about.

It's About to Get Real

In the previous chapter, we learned how generational knowledge and generational wealth can positively impact a young adult's financial journey. As First-Gen, we don't get a shortcut. We have to trek through the muck all on our own and learn the fundamentals of money management that were never taught to us at home. Many of us start life in the negative and are weighed down by debt, while others get the advantage of skipping ahead and start building their financial future.

Additionally, we have to unlearn negative money mindsets and habits we learned from our parents because some of these beliefs can set us back in our finances. Our culture and upbringing shape how we show up and interact with money, so it's important that we take time to explore that intersection.

But first, let's dig deeper and understand why this financial literacy gap exists in our community in the first place.

SCHOOL DOESN'T TEACH PERSONAL FINANCE

In K–12, they'll teach us the periodic table in chemistry or the Pythagorean theorem in math class. But nobody teaches us the stuff that *really* matters, like how to create a budget or how to understand a credit card statement. They don't even teach you this stuff in college! I graduated with a degree in economics, and I still didn't learn how to manage money. Make it make sense!

According to Next Gen Personal Finance's 2022 State of Financial Education Report, only one in every four students has access to personal finance education in their high school.[1] This means that 75 percent of high school graduates from our mighty public education system may not have basic money management skills.

Understanding how money works is a critical life skill. This is not the Stone Age. We don't get to barter with sticks and nuts huddled in a dark, cold cave with fig leaves covering our vag anymore. We need money to pay for our housing, health insurance, groceries,

---

1   "NGPF'S 2022 State of Financial Education Report." Next Gen Personal Finance. January 1, 2022. https://doi.org/https://d3f7q2msm2165u.cloudfront.net/aaa-content/user/files/Files/NGPFAnnualReport_2022.pdf.

and all of life's necessities. And it's important that we know how to administer it and use it wisely.

It truly is a disservice to throw young adults into the "real world" without at least a basic understanding of the fundamentals. Especially when the student debt crisis disproportionately affects Black, Indigenous, and other people of color,[2] who not only carry more debt than their peers and don't have the knowledge to understand how it works, but they also struggle to secure equal-paying jobs so they *can* pay off their debts.

OUR PARENTS LIVED IN SURVIVAL MODE

The lack of financial literacy in school affects all students, but at least the students with parents who have generational knowledge can be taught some basics at home. That's not the experience of the children of immigrants.

Our parents lived in survival mode. Immigrant life is not easy. As new immigrants, they had to leave everything and everyone they knew and loved in their home country to start a new life in the US and give their children an *opportunity* for a better life. They had to learn a new language, navigate cultural differences, and assimilate to the American way of life. Their biggest priority was putting food on the table and feeding their family on a minimum-wage salary.

Our parents didn't have the luxury to even begin to think about how to hack the system and make it work in their favor to get ahead. *They were just trying to get by.* Their only goal was to survive in this new system, not to learn how to thrive in it. For them,

2   Williams, Ward. "Student Loan Debt by Race: Students of Color Face Greater Risks When It Comes to Educational Debt." Investopedia, February 27, 2023. https://www.investopedia.com/student-loan-debt-by-race-5193137.

just paying the bills on time in a foreign country was a win. A lot of them didn't have the privilege or financial means to plan for life in the next twenty, ten, or even five years. Their biggest priority was surviving that month and hoping they could do it again the month after that.

OUR PARENTS MISTRUST FINANCIAL SYSTEMS

Another barrier that can affect your family's ability to build wealth in this country is their mistrust of banks. If your parents immigrated from a country with a poorly regulated financial system, they probably don't trust financial institutions. My parents had terrible banking experiences with Mexican banks. Both my parents have felt cheated and lied to by the Mexican financial system, and they've carried over those negative feelings of mistrust to this country.

For years, my dad kept his life savings, about $45,000, debajo de su colchón. I tirelessly begged him to take his money to the bank to keep it safe. I would challenge him and ask him, "What if the house burns down? What if someone breaks in? And then what? There goes all your hard-earned money." He stubbornly replied that he'd rather take his chances with all those things happening than trust a bank with his money. The mistrust is *real*.

Although the US financial system is one of the most regulated institutions in the world, it hasn't done a great job of earning the trust of the immigrant community. Recently, I was a panelist at a summit with the National Credit Union Administration, where we discussed how I'm leveraging social media to reach minorities and access the unbanked, meaning those individuals who don't own a checking or savings account. I spoke of how the industry is riddled with confusing financial jargon that intimidates the average English-speaking American. We hear foreign terms like "annual percentage yield" and "par value" but get little to no explanation of what these words actually mean.

The jargon is even *more* inaccessible to an immigrant who speaks little English and doesn't have a full mastery of the language. It's one of the reasons "finfluencers" are so popular on social media these days. We speak in plain English and are much more approachable and relatable than a stuffy suit at a bank. We create safe spaces for people to learn.

To make matters worse, financial institutions don't hire enough bilingual staff in customer-facing roles that can service them in their native language. According to the Certified Financial Planner Board, in 2022, only 2.9 percent of CFPs (Certified Financial Planners) were Hispanic.[3] Most can't even offer an interpreter line to help. This leaves non-English speakers feeling embarrassed and vulnerable at a time when they need guidance and support from financial professionals. No wonder we got stuck translating for our parents!

A few lifetimes ago, I worked as a claims adjuster for a car insurance company. My job was to help people process auto claims and help them get their cars fixed after an accident. If you had a fender bender, I was the annoying insurance lady on the phone who asked you all the details about how it happened. I still remember the big sigh of relief I'd hear on the other end of the phone once I informed a Spanish-speaking customer that I, too, spoke Spanish—"Claro que hablo español. ¡A su servicio!" They'd instantly tell me they were relieved I could help them in Spanish.

---

3   "CFP Board Exceeds 95,000 CFP® Professionals, Increases Gender and Racial Diversity of Financial Planning Profession." CPF. January 19, 2023. https://doi.org/https://www.cfp.net/news/2023/01/cfp-board-exceeds-95000-cfp-professionals#:~:text=The%20number%20of%20Hispanic%20CFP,%C2%AE%20professionals%20increased%20by%206.7%25.

Bilingual speakers make people feel safe. They help foster an inclusive banking experience. They can make customers feel seen as they're able to speak to them in the language they're most comfortable in. They're also better able to build rapport which improves the customer service experience and increases the customer retention rate. It's hard to build trust and form a true connection when the extent of someone's Spanish is only "un poe-kee-toe."

And lastly, the financial planning industry is broken. It doesn't prioritize the interests of low-net-worth individuals. A financial planner is a trusted adviser who can help people meet their long-term money goals. They provide expert guidance on money matters related to investments, taxes, retirement, and estate planning. These are all things that, if managed wisely, can improve our financial wellness and even make us rich over time.

Most financial planners or advisers are paid a percentage of their client's investment portfolio. For example, let's say a client has an investment portfolio worth $500,000. If they earn a 1 percent management fee for handling that client's portfolio, they'll earn a $5,000 annual fee. The higher their client's net worth, the more money they make. Which naturally incentivizes them only to seek out high-net-worth individuals. Most financial advisers won't even take you on as a client until you have at least $100,000 in assets. Any less than that isn't worth their time and effort under the current model. When the median Hispanic household only has $36,100 in wealth,[4] it's no surprise why our community is overlooked and underserved.

4   Bhutta, Neil, Andrew C. Chang, Lisa J. Dettling, Joanne W. Hsu, and Julia Hewitt. "FEDS Notes: Disparities in Wealth by Race and Ethnicity in the 2019 Survey of Consumer Finances." Federal Reserve. September 28, 2020. https://www.federalreserve.gov/econres/notes/feds-notes/disparities-in-wealth-by-race-and-ethnicity-in-the-2019-survey-of-consumer-finances-20200928.html.

THEIR IMMIGRATION STATUS

If your parents are undocumented, that could be another reason why they're disengaged from the US financial system. A lot of undocumented immigrants fear that if they get on the government's radar, they can risk deportation. For them, it's better to play it safe and avoid banks altogether. (BTW, your undocumented parents *can* participate in the US financial system by applying for an ITIN with the IRS. ITIN stands for Individual Taxpayer Identification Number. With an ITIN, they can do things like open a checking account or apply for a home loan. The IRS doesn't enforce immigration laws and is completely separate from the US Department of Homeland Security.)

If they live in fear of deportation, this fear might also keep them from holding their assets in the United States. They may think, what's the point in keeping money here if they can get deported tomorrow? Will their money stay stuck here? They'd rather have it with them where they can see it instead of risk losing it.

Individualistic Versus Collectivist Cultures

Now that we've covered some of the reasons why our parents are unbanked and haven't fully participated in the US financial system let's talk about how they were able to get by without it. This is largely because our Latine families operate within a collectivist money culture. But first, let's discuss how an individualistic culture manages money.

An individualistic culture *prioritizes the needs of the individual over the needs of others*. This is how money is managed in the US. In this culture, people are considered good with money if they are self-reliant, independent, and autonomous. When it comes to money, you prioritize what's best for your financial needs. Not what's best for others.

Someone needs help with money, but you can't swing it? Too bad, they should have made better choices. "I'm not going to jeopardize my financial well-being over you! I have to focus on my own life."

By the same token, if you're ever stuck in a financial pickle, you're on your own. You pull yourself from the good ol' bootstraps and figure it out. You got yourself into this mess. Now get yourself out. You don't immediately turn to others for help. As a very last resort, you can go to your loved ones to ask for help with money, but that comes with shame and embarrassment. According to this money culture, it's embarrassing to ask for help or to let others know you're struggling financially. It's a sign of weakness that you aren't self-sufficient with your finances. If you need money, you charge it on a credit card or take out a bank loan. Your worth is determined by how independent you are with your money matters. The fewer people involved, the better.

On the other end of the spectrum are collectivist cultures. Most Latine communities operate under this type of culture. *A collectivist culture prioritizes the needs of others over your own.* You're expected to be obedient, self-sacrificing, and put the group's needs before your individual needs when help is needed.

Someone in your family needs some extra cash? You drop what you're doing now to help. You don't have the money to help? No importa. Being a good family member means you're there for your family when they call—no questions asked. You figure out a way to show up for them. Any deviation from that signals you're selfish and not a dependable family member.

Similarly, if you need financial support, the first place you turn to is family. You don't need a bank. Because that's what family is for, they're there for you when you need them the most. If others loan you money, it's a sign that you're loved and trusted enough to pay it back. In this money culture, your worth is determined by how committed you are to helping your family get out of financial hardships, no matter the cost.

Do you see the money culture clash?

The way money is handled in both these cultures is so different that when the two meet, there is typically some conflict.

This culture clash comes up a lot on one of my favorite reality TV shows called *90 Day Fiancé*. The show is a series that follows the journey of couples bringing their foreign boyfriend or girlfriend to the US to get married and build a life in America. Typically, you'll see an American meeting the love of their life abroad in a developing country like Nigeria or Brazil. The show captures the couples as they navigate visa issues, adjust to married life in the US, and deal with family conflict.

One of the reocurring themes is how they navigate money as a couple and with their extended family abroad. One of the couples who struggles the most with clashing money cultures is Chantel from Atlanta, GA, and Pedro from the Dominican Republic.

Chantel and Pedro are in their early twenties and just getting started in life. They live in a small, cramped apartment while Chantel is putting herself through nursing school, and Pedro is working full-time at a warehouse.

Although Pedro works a minimum-wage job, in a week, he makes more than what his family back in the DR can make in a month. While Pedro is living a more prosperous life in the States, his mother and younger (adult) sister are still struggling to get by in the Dominican Republic. Since Pedro is the only son in his family, he feels it's his responsibility to support them financially. It's how he was raised. His mom and sister frequently remind him of his duty and ask that he transfer them a monthly allowance and send them gifts, like new TVs or new clothes. When he tells them he's low on cash, they guilt him into sending money anyway.

This is how things are done in the DR, a collectivist money culture. Pedro is proud to be in a position to help and feels it's the least he can do for his mom, who did everything for him as a single mother. He thinks it would be selfish not to help and is willing to sacrifice his financial progress to be there for those he loves.

But his American fiancée, Chantel, isn't okay with this arrangement. Chantel feels they are in no position to help. She knows Pedro isn't making a ton of money. She's not making any income as a nursing student. As a new couple, they have plans to move out of their small apartment and buy their first home. They want to start a family soon. She doesn't feel they can meet their own financial goals and life plans if they're giving away money to support Pedro's family abroad.

Chantel and Pedro argue a lot because she thinks he should stop sending his extended family money and instead focus on their plans as a newlywed couple. She feels bad that his family isn't in a better financial situation but doesn't feel it's her responsibility to fix their money problems. As an American, she abides by the individualistic money culture, where her finances are more important than someone else's.

It's entertaining to watch people's drama play out on TV, but it's not as fun once it happens to you. I'm all too familiar with this feeling. It's confusing, stressful, and isolating.

A Bicultural Approach to Managing Money

As First-Gen, we have a bicultural upbringing, whether you're Mexican American, Puerto Rican American, Salvadorian American, Colombian American, and so on. We inherit our parents' collectivist money values by default, but as we set deeper roots in America, the individualistic money values start to seep in. Similar to how Pedro and Chantel have to navigate two money cultures, we have to learn to do the same—hopefully without the intense drama of reality TV.

So which is right? The way your family does things? Or the way the typical American handles money? I don't think one culture is better than the other. They're just different. Both have their pros and cons. IMO, one is too selfish, but the other is too selfless. Call me Goldilocks, but I believe there's something in the middle that's *just* right.

If you want to improve your relationship with money and learn how to build wealth, you're going to have to redefine which of these money values works best for you. You're going to have to challenge cultural norms, keep what serves you, and leave what doesn't. Or, as they say, eat the fruit and spit out the seeds.

Cultura & Cash will guide you through that process. More on this later in the boundary section of this chapter.

What Limiting Beliefs Do You Have About Money?

Now that we discussed some of the systemic and cultural barriers we're up against in our financial journey let's take it a step further and cover some of the most common limiting money beliefs that plague our community. Yes, I said plague!

This isn't an exhaustive list, but it's the top three most common ones I've seen from past money-coaching clients. If you identify with any of the mindsets below, it's critical that you are intentional in unlearning these beliefs as soon as you can. Not to be dramatic, but these beliefs can make you subconsciously repel money and can block you from receiving it. It's a big reason why I've included affirmations at the beginning of each chapter, to reprogram your mind to embrace a positive money mindset.

HARD WORK EQUALS MONEY

First one up is the belief that you must work hard to earn money. In the Latine community, there's a strong belief that if you work hard, everything will work itself out, and you will achieve success. We're conditioned to work hard and keep our head down. In our community, it's a sense of pride to be the hardest worker in the room. "Nobody can deny hard work" is what we hear growing up. Working hard was our parents' only option and all they knew.

Working hard can be great and can give us a sense of accomplishment when we meet our goals. But the belief that you **must** work hard to earn money is not true. You can make money while you sleep through the power of compound interest and investing. You can make money by collecting rental income while you're sipping a Michelada on vacation. As a matter of fact, I'm making money right now while I'm writing this book through my investment accounts and my digital courses. I also know an industry colleague who made $20,000 in a day from affiliate income after her interview with a digital publication hit the internet. There's nothing hard about chatting with a reporter for thirty minutes and collecting a $20,000 check. I'll take that ease any day!

You do not have to be burning from both ends of the candle to earn money. If you believe you need to work hard to make money, that's what you'll manifest—burnout and unnecessary stress.

Hard work alone is not enough. What you need is a plan and the tools to execute that plan. The real flex is *working smarter* by learning how to make money-savvy moves to take care of past you, current you, and future you. We'll cover how to do this with my First Gen Five framework in the rest of this book.

If you identify with the narrative that you must work hard to make money, try this affirmation: Money flows easily and effortlessly to me. Put your hands on your chest, take a couple of deep breaths to center yourself, and say it out loud right now while you're reading this book: *Money flows easily and effortlessly to me.*

Don't ignore me. Do it with me. Speak every word with confidence and intention. In the same way that you'd state the sky is blue or the grass is green: *Money flows easily and effortlessly to me.*

the affirmations throughout this book.

ABOUT FINANCIAL TRAUMA, ANXIETY, AND SHAME

Although affirmations are great tools to reframe negative money mindsets, you can't manifest your way out of financial trauma. If you've experienced severe financial distress like being unhoused, living in a toxic home due to money conflict, or are still punishing yourself for past money mistakes, you may be experiencing financial trauma, financial anxiety, or financial shame. If left unresolved, these emotional wounds can have a negative impact on how you interact with your finances. If you resonate with this, please seek guidance from a mental health professional to help you heal your relationship with money. Visit latinxtherapy.com or cliniciansofcolor.org to fincd a therapist near you.

A SCARCITY MINDSET

A scarcity mindset is the belief that no matter what we do, there will never be enough. "What's the point in trying? This is as good as it's going to get for me." It's almost like we don't feel we are deserving of financial ease. We have feelings that we aren't enough, or that being good with money is not for us, and that our path is always going to be one of struggle.

My mom used to tell me, "What's the point in paying off debt? You'll always have debt." Says who? I've lived debt free for three-plus years. Lots of people live debt free for much longer. You don't have to be a one-percenter to live a debt-free life.

I saw this theme come up recently in one of my favorite rom-coms, Jennifer Lopez's *Maid in Manhattan*. In the movie, her good friend encourages her to apply for a management role at the hotel where she works as a housekeeper. JLo's character says, "Give me a break, all right? They're not going to make a maid a manager." Scarcity mindset.

Her friend replies, "Why not? Today is a new day. Anything is possible. You know what I'm sayin'?" Abundance mindset.

Scarcity mindset keeps us from even trying!

You are deserving. You are enough. Money is abundant and is yours for the taking. Money is a tool that allows you to live a life on your terms. The more money you have, the more freely you can give and support those you love.

To counteract this limiting money belief, try this affirmation: I welcome unlimited wealth and abundance into my life.

JUST BE GRATEFUL

One of the core values of the Latine culture is to be grateful for what we have—to be *agradecidas* for a roof over our head, food in our fridge, and running water. We're encouraged to be grateful for love, health, family, and opportunities. It's a beautiful value. It anchors us to the present and helps give us perspective into how much we have compared to others or a past version of ourselves.

But sometimes, this attitude of just being grateful can breed complacency and can keep you playing small, which affects how we manage our money.

When you aspire for more, you may hear, "Be grateful for your job. I never got to work a nice office job like you," or "Why aren't you happy with what you have? Some people have it a lot worse."

We can be grateful for what we have and still aspire for more. We should desire more than the bare minimum. It doesn't make you greedy to want more. Gratitude and ambition can both exist at the same time.

A few years ago, I told my aunt I was preparing notes for a meeting with my supervisor to discuss my pay. I told her I'd been working extra hours at my job since my coworker was on paternity leave and wanted a salary increase for the additional responsibilities I'd picked up. She said, "But aren't you happy with what you're getting paid? You should be grateful for your job. You work at a great company." All those things can be true, but that doesn't mean that I didn't deserve a raise.

And my boss agreed with me. I ignored my aunt's well-intentioned, bad advice and got a raise during a company salary freeze. Just "being grateful" would have kept me underpaid and overworked!

When you feel that you've made it further than your parents ever have, it's easy to feel that your current money situation is enough and you shouldn't aspire for more. You may even experience what some people call "First Gen Guilt" and feel conflicted about having the opportunity to achieve more, knowing that your parents never will.

But remember, this is exactly why our parents came to this country! So we could do better than them and accomplish so much more. They immigrated here to give us the opportunity to have a better life. Our family didn't bring us here to play small and settle for less. And since we have a different starting line, we'll need more money and resources to secure our financial future, our parents, and that of future generations. We can't afford to play small.

If you resonate with this limiting money belief, try this affirmation: More money is good. More money is safe. The more I receive, the freer I feel.

And lastly, if you identify with the feelings of First Gen guilt, a therapist can help you practice self-compassion and overcome negative self-talk.

ACTIVITY: PAUSE AND REFLECT

A moment here to pause and reflect on whether the money narratives you've been fed in the past are helping or holding you back on your financial journey. If it's not serving you, leave it behind. ¡No te conviene!

Unlearn Limiting Beliefs with Compassion

If any of the limiting beliefs I covered resonated with you, I hope that instead of feeling frustrated with your family, you feel a sense of compassion. A lot of them adopted these beliefs as survival skills in this capitalist society. The system was not created for low-income immigrants to thrive in.

Their opportunities were limited, which left them with no other choice but to work hard. Their low-paying jobs made money scarce, leading to their scarcity mindset. They had to be grateful for the bare necessities; they didn't have the means to dream beyond that. That's been their reality.

I believe a lot of our parents did the best they could with what they had. Their sacrifice to immigrate here gave us the opportunity to have so much more than what was ever available to them. But it's important to note that these limiting money beliefs will work against you if they go unnoticed. Know they exist and how they can manifest, and learn to release them to improve your relationship with money.

Immigrant Money Habits That Keep Us Broke

In this chapter, we've covered the financial literacy gap in our community, our immigrant parents' mistrust of the financial system, how our collectivist culture affects our money, and how some limiting money beliefs hold us back from living a life of financial abundance.

I also want to acknowledge the role systemic barriers play in Latines' ability to build wealth. A long history of colonialism in Latin America, discriminatory immigration policies in the US, unequal access to higher education, redlining to gatekeep homeownership from Black and Brown communities,[5] and the pay and wealth gap have made it more difficult to attain wealth and achieve financial success. All these barriers have an impact on our finances, and according to the Federal Reserve, Hispanic households hold 20 percent less wealth than the median white household. Our people work too hard to have so little. We need real systemic change to overturn discriminatory practices that keep our community from trailing behind others.

But let's be real. Although we can't blame the individual for systemic problems, we have to admit that our community can also mismanage the money that we do have. And since this book is about helping *individuals* be wiser with their finances, I need to expose some immigrant money habits that keep us broke—so you don't make those same mistakes. A lot of these toxic money patterns are normalized as just being a part of our cultura but they can really have a negative impact on our financial progress.

THROWING EXTRAVAGANT PARTIES

It's no secret that we know how to have a good time and party! We spare no expense when it comes to having great-tasting food, endless drinks, lively music, and beautiful party decor. But do we need to spend thousands of dollars (that we don't have) on a one-year-old's *bautizo*? Or go into debt for a three-year-old's *piñata*? Extravagant parties are an unnecessary expense when we have bigger fish to fry, like paying down our debt, building savings, or investing for our future. If you've checked off those boxes and have the disposable

---

5   Ray, Rashawn, Andre M. Perry, David Harshbarger, Samantha Elizondo, and Alexandra Gibbons. "Homeownership, Racial Segregation, and Policy Solutions to Racial Wealth Equity." Brookings, (2021). https://www.brookings.edu/articles/homeownership-racial-segregation-and-policies-for-racial-wealth-equity/.

income to have elaborate parties and want to throw a Kardashian-style bash—knock yourself out! But until then, we have to be more mindful of party expenses.

When I was a teenager, my parents threw me a *quinceañera for my fifteenth birthday*. I'm their only daughter, and they made sure this party would be lit. They paid a seamstress to sew me a custom sage green sequined ball gown that fit me like a glove. They hired the best DJ in town to play the perfect mix of music: Ying Yang Twins for my teenage friends and me to twerk to and La Sonora Dinamita for the *doñas to dance cumbias all night long*. The event hall was decorated with majestic and elaborate floral centerpieces (which, of course, everyone took home at the end of the night). We had a videographer document my special day, and every now and then, I'll rewatch the video to relive those happy memories.

I'm thankful my parents threw me a party to celebrate my milestone birthday. But as I've matured and learned about finances, I wish they'd had a more modest party and been smarter with their money. They didn't have the means to throw me this extravagant party, and they got into credit card debt to pay for it. It cost them $15,000—plus interest.

If they had used $5,000 of that money for a smaller party, invested the other $10,000 in the stock market, and never added another dime, in thirty years, it could have grown to $100,626.57 (assuming an 8 percent annual rate of return, which we will define later). This is ten times more than their original investment of $10,000. Let that sink in.

Although I had a lot of fun backing it up to Petey Pablo's "Freek-a-Leek," I did not get $100,000 worth of fun. That's money they could have used toward a safer and more fruitful retirement for them both.

There is nothing wrong with having a party and celebrating life's special occasions. And if you come from a history of hardship, it's not hard to see why someone would choose to live in the moment and spend extravagantly on parties. It's not a rational decision but an emotional one. But these celebrations shouldn't come at the expense of our overall financial wellness. Instead of having over-the-top parties, embrace a budget-friendly event that allows us to build memories without derailing our finances and future life plans.

VALUING STUFF OVER ASSETS

Now this one isn't exclusive to our community. In any capitalist society, you're going to be bombarded with marketing campaigns promising to make you feel prettier, healthier, smarter, and cooler— if only you buy their product, of course. They've convinced us that our worth is determined by the stuff we have, whether it's the newest iPhone or a new electric car model.

This can lead us to buy more stuff to show others, "Look what I've got. I made it!" Meanwhile this same person doesn't have any real assets to show for themselves. Assets include things like cash savings, investment accounts, and real estate. Assets hold or increase in value over time.

Traditional personal finance books call this phenomenon having a "big hat, no cattle." Meaning you see a rancher with a big hat and assume he is wealthy because he looks the part, only to find out he doesn't own a ranch or any cattle. Big hat, no cattle.

This topic came up recently with my dad the other day when we had a serious conversation about his retirement. He's nearing retirement age, and I told him I want to proactively plan for his next stage in life together. His current home is much larger than what he really needs. It's a lot of space for just him. I asked him to start thinking about downsizing his home to save money and have extra funds to use toward retirement.

He agreed that downsizing could only help, but then he went on to assure me that his finances were fine. To prove he was doing well, he showed me a closet full of $500 cowboy hats and expensive cowboy boots. He said all his clothes are good quality and he doesn't wear rags. He reminded me that he owns four cars (all paid for in cash) and that he's doing just fine. In his eyes, he is wealthy.

"¡Apá! Cowboy hats aren't assets!" I groaned with frustration.

Like a lot of the Latine community, my dad feels that the stuff he has, whether it's what he wears or drives, demonstrates his wealth. It doesn't. He can't pay the cost of utilities or medical expenses in retirement with cowboy hats. It's just stuff. Stuff doesn't increase your wealth or make you richer. Assets do. To thrive financially, we need to learn to buy assets and use investments to increase our wealth and our family's legacy. More about this in Chapter 7.

GIVING MONEY YOU DON'T HAVE TO FAMILY

Sometimes, our strong family values lead us to give more money to our family than we can truly afford. We are raised to believe that to be a good daughter, we must give money freely and unconditionally—no matter the cost. We're conditioned to believe our value is rooted in our ability to be obedient and agreeable. Like we discussed earlier in this chapter, these are strong collectivist values.

This could look like you cosigning for your cousin to buy a car but jeopardizing your credit score if they stop making payments. Or overspending on Christmas presents to show up to Noche Buena like Santa Claus to demonstrate your love but getting hit with a huge credit card bill you can't afford to pay back in January. Or giving your college student a monthly allowance to help with expenses while you're living paycheck to paycheck and neglecting your retirement fund.

A family member of mine, let's call her Ana, used to frequently pull money from her small retirement account to help our extended family with money. Our extended family owned a small business in México, and because it was poorly managed, they frequently ran into financial troubles. Since business financing isn't as accessible in México, they constantly turned to Ana for help. Even though Ana didn't have any savings to loan them money, they knew she had a retirement plan she could pull money from. She didn't think twice about withdrawing the money; after all, they were family, and they were in need.

But this came at the expense of her retirement. Ana is now nearing sixty and doesn't have a cent to her name in her retirement plan. Because of this, she's going to have to work well into her old age, with a bad knee, because she gave away money she didn't have and ignored her own financial needs.

Some may argue that Ana did this out of love and concern. But she needs to practice that same love and concern for her finances too. So should you.

We were raised to think that if we can take care of other people first and ourselves last, we're good people. We're good daughters. We're good sisters. Good nietas. But in reality, you have to take care of yourself first so you can be more generous and give to those you love later.

To be clear, my message isn't to discourage people from helping their families. I love my family too, and I feel a great sense of pride for helping them when I can.

When I was in college, I saw post-grad life through rose-colored glasses. I thought I'd live the good life in a swanky high-rise city apartment, driving a nice car, vacationing whenever I wanted, enjoying fabulous dinners with friends while paying for my family's bills, and buying my mom a vacation home (on a whopping $45,000 salary, mind you).

But I very quickly learned that that's not how the real world works. You can have all those things, but they take time to build, especially when you're just starting out as a young adult. This means that right now, you have to make choices and understand your money boundaries.

If supporting family is important to you, let's come up with a plan to lend them a hand—without derailing your finances. Understand the opportunity cost of providing this support and how it will affect your ability to make progress with your own finances. And when your financial well-being is at risk, learn to get comfortable setting boundaries and saying no.

When to Help and When to Set Financial Boundaries

Boundaries are a tricky subject in our comunidad. Our families are so close-knit that boundaries feel almost foreign to us. Familismo is a central Latine cultural value, and it makes us value the importance of strong family loyalty and closeness to our family.

But a younger generation is starting to learn how important and beneficial healthy boundaries can be with those we love. We are normalizing boundaries when it comes to our body, self-care, and our parenting style. Long gone are the days when our family gets a free pass to comment on our bodies and whether we've gained or lost weight. We no longer force our children to kiss or hug an extended family member if a child doesn't want to, even if it offends someone. We're learning to effectively and respectfully say no to yet another weekend carne asada when we feel we need to rest and prioritize our self-care.

Healthy boundaries are not selfish. And our money needs boundaries too!

After years and years of navigating financial conflict with my family, I came up with a process to decide whether I should provide financial support to my family or set a boundary. I call it the Quiero y Puedo approach. My philosophy is to give freely if you *want* to and if you are *able to*.

The Quiero y Puedo Approach

DO YOU WANT TO?

NO — set the Boundary

YES! — CAN YOU AFFORD IT?

NO — set the Boundary

YES! — PAT YOURSELF ON THE BACK FOR DOING IT ON YOUR TERMS ACCORDING TO YOUR VALUES.

#1. QUIERO
DO YOU WANT TO?

Why do you want to give money to family? You'll need to do some inner work here and be honest with your response.

Are you doing it out of gratitude and to show appreciation to those who supported you in the past? Or are you doing it because you feel pressured or guilted into it because it's what you're "supposed to do"?

A lot of First Gen feel indebted to their family for the sacrifices their parents made for them. And it's a valid feeling. Our families gave up a lot to immigrate here. They gave up their home and language and moved away from loved ones to give us better opportunities. It's important to acknowledge these sacrifices and be thankful for all our parents gave us.

But we also have to understand that these were *choices* your parents made as adults. Your parents made those choices out of love, not so that they could come back years later to knock on your door and collect a debt owed to them. Accept what they freely gave to you. Feel thankful, not indebted.

If you give money to others out of guilt, pressure, or fear of receiving backlash and not because it's what you truly want, you're people-pleasing. You may be people-pleasing because you fear rejection or don't want to disappoint others. Eventually, this may lead to resenting your loved ones. It feels much better to give freely on your terms—porque te nace. If you choose to give, do it out of love, gratitude, and appreciation.

And if you choose not to, that's fine too. Nobody is a good or bad person because they choose to help family or not. My friend, let's call him Alfredo, doesn't financially support his immigrant Filipina mother even though he's a millionaire and runs a very successful business. He grew up in an unsafe home with a family who struggled with alcohol and gambling addictions. His childhood was traumatic. He's made the decision not to provide financial support to his mom.

Some may judge him as selfish or ungrateful. I say it's none of our business. We all have our unique family dynamic and history, and we get to decide what's in alignment with our values and best for our family and finances. Consider this next time you're deciding whether you should set a financial boundary.

#2. Y PUEDO
ARE YOU ABLE TO? (BUT *REALLY* ABLE TO?)

If you've decided that helping family is a priority to you, amazing! It can be a beautiful thing to give freely to those you love, especially when it's on your terms. Now that we've established that you want to provide this aid ask yourself: Are you financially able to?

Are your finances in order to support other people? Do you have a strong emergency fund that will protect you in case you lose your job next month? Do you have your debt under control and a plan to pay it off soon? Do you have extra savings set aside for other financial goals, like having money to replace your car when it's time for a new one? Are you making steady progress toward your retirement plan? Do you have disposable income available to you that won't require you to go into debt to help?

If you answered yes to all of these questions, you go, Glen Coco! You have all your financial ducks in a row and should have no problem providing that additional support to those who matter to you. It's a great place to be in!

If you answered no to some of the questions above, that's okay! That's why you're reading this book, to learn how to improve your finances and get in a position to give freely. It doesn't mean you can't help family at all. You can still help them but in a smaller capacity. Just like flight attendants teach you during their safety demonstrations, you have to put on your oxygen mask first before you help the person next to you.

At the end of every following chapter, we'll discuss ways we can support (or set boundaries with) our family when discussing financial emergencies, providing recurring allowances, taking on debt for them, allowing them to use our credit, or helping with retirement. Use the Quiero y Puedo approach to help guide you toward the decision that feels right for you.

¡Pero aguas!

Don't say I didn't warn you! Boundaries work great in theory but are harder to execute in real life. In Latine families, setting boundaries can be like choosing violence.

In a perfect world, you'd lovingly set the boundary with your parents and hear, "No problem, mija, I understand," and move on to the next topic. But back to our collectivist and familismo values, saying anything but an immediate yes can be seen as the ultimate sign of betrayal. Because if family isn't there for you, who will be?

Setting boundaries can lead to arguments and additional stress around money. You can be called selfish, greedy, coda, cuenta chiles, and a mal agradecida, just to name a few. You can be told you've forgotten your roots or that you're acting like white people do. Saying no or saying not right now doesn't make you a bad daughter, but it will be hard to convince them otherwise because it's instilled in their culture.

Stay strong in your boundaries, and don't cave under external pressure. It's going to be hard. You'll feel guilty for doing it at first. But you are in control of setting your boundaries, and only you get to decide what happens with your money. I'll say it again—healthy boundaries are not selfish. They are an act of self-love. Like anything else, they get easier and easier the more you practice them.

It's not easy to be the first in your family to break generational patterns. It's a process. But doing this work is necessary to set up future generations for financial success. I know you can do it.

I've given money to family out of guilt when I was too broke to do it. I've also given money to family on my terms when I truly wanted to and when I had the extra money to help. And I can assure you, it feels much more empowering and freeing to do it the second way.

You've Got This

We've covered a lot of heavy topics in this chapter. We've talked about the systemic and cultural barriers our community faces when managing money. We've also explored some of the common limiting money beliefs and immigrant money behaviors that keep us broke. Lastly, we talked about how difficult but necessary financial boundaries can be in our money journey. You've made it through the toughest sections of this book. You should feel proud of yourself!

These uncomfortable conversations were necessary to truly understand how our cultura affects how we interact with money. And now you'll be better prepared to identify and tackle these issues when they happen in real life and make wiser money choices.

These are all topics Privileged Patty and Average Amy rarely have to worry about. Our road is a little harder, but we're smart, hardworking, and resourceful. And with the right guidance, we can do this!

How to Move Forward Toward Financial Success

And now, to the solutions! Did you think I was going to bring up all these problems and money traumas and leave you hanging? No ma'am!

In the remaining chapters, I'll share strategies for how you can close the gap with your finances and set yourself up for financial success—without generational wealth. We'll cover more general, practical, and actionable money tips you can use to get your finances in a better place. It will be the how-to portion of this book. It should feel much more lighthearted than the beginning sections, I promise!

We'll dive deep into my First Gen Five framework, where I'll teach you the top five financial pillars you should focus on first to set up your financial foundation: emergency funds, budgets, debt, credit score, and investing. With a little storytelling and a side of chisme, I'll share money lessons of how these pillars personally affected me as a young adult, and what you can do to avoid my mistakes or achieve similar success.

We'll begin with a chapter on the importance of having savings and creating our safety net, especially when it comes to emergencies. Let's begin our work!

CHAPTER 3

EMERGENCY FUNDS: YOUR LIFEBOAT WHEN SH*T HITS THE FAN

I deserve to be free of financial worries.

The office felt lively and buzzed with financial professionals scurrying off to their next client conference call. We had a friendly receptionist who welcomed important stakeholders to large meeting rooms with big mahogany desks and expensive leather chairs. Looks like the VIP conference room with an ocean view is occupied again. That means our head honchos are busy working their magic to win some new business at a client pitch meeting.

This was the scene as I was working at an investment consulting firm in San Diego, CA. I reported to a manager who was all business and had an impressive Ivy League education. If there was a last-minute client office tour, my colleagues and I quickly put on the suit jackets we kept at our desks and slapped on a smile to shake hands and schmooze our important guests. This job was by far the fanciest one I'd had yet. It felt and looked nothing like the small agricultural border town I grew up in.

I finally felt like the corporate baddie I had always aspired to be. I thought, "This is exactly why I went to school! This is why I took thousands of dollars of student debt to go to college. This is why I sacrificed so many late nights studying for econ finals and writing long research papers. To work at a fancy office job my parents could be proud of."

The Overachieving Team Player

I was excited about the opportunity to grow my career at this company. I wanted to make a good impression, and I wanted to be viewed by management as a strong performer. To add more pressure, I was the only Latina in an investment role, and I felt I had to work twice as hard to prove I belonged in the sea of white, mostly male faces in my office. The pressure was on.

That's why when my boss told me that I'd have to take on additional work while they found a replacement for an employee leaving the firm, I happily agreed.

Of course, I could handle it! Sure, I was already working a full schedule on my deliverables, but losing Ernie was a blow to our small team of three. That wasn't my bosses' fault, my team's, or our clients'. And I wanted to be a team player. I'd do whatever it took to deliver our client reports without disruption. I felt ready for the challenge and was eager to prove my worth.

But my 5 p.m.-evenings quickly turned to long 10 p.m.-nights. Not only was I tasked with picking up the majority of Ernie's reports, but I also inherited his most complex and time-consuming deliverables. To keep up, I worked around the clock crunching numbers on Microsoft Excel, going late into the night, often until 10 p.m. or midnight. One time I even worked until 2 a.m. on a Friday evening.

I knew these hours weren't reasonable, but I felt I was doing what I had to do to earn my stripes as a loyal employee willing to do anything for the firm. Even if it meant I had to sacrifice my work-life balance.

Running on Fumes

Well, it turns out I girl bossed a little too close to the sun. After a couple of weeks, the unsustainable hours started to take a toll on my body. I was so wired from all the late-night $1 McCafé iced coffees that I struggled to turn off my brain and sleep when I needed to. A lot of times, I'd get home around 11 p.m. but would toss and turn until close to 2 a.m. Then I'd wake up at 6:30 a.m. and do it all over again. There was no room to exercise, cook a nutritious meal, or spend quality time with the people I loved. I was surviving on junk food, cheap coffee, and a few hours of rest. I was putting in long hours at the office, but the work kept piling on.

This unhealthy lifestyle and my high-stress work environment worsened my preexisting anxiety and made it even harder to sleep. I'd lie in bed late at night, feeling restless and short of breath. My anxiety made me feel like I had a twenty-pound dumbbell crushing my chest. I had to remind myself to breathe constantly. I had an old Xanax prescription at home, so I started doubling and tripling my dosage just to fall asleep and get a couple of hours of rest.

My friends and family started worrying about me when they noticed my sudden weight loss. I'd dropped ten pounds in a month. During a phone call, my uncle picked up the high stress in my voice and told me I sounded manic. He and my aunt urged me to scale back on work and prioritize my health.

At this point, I didn't care about impressing my employer anymore. I knew the long work hours weren't good for me, but I had a lot of reports to get done. My boss knew I was working late too and didn't care. I emailed progress reports late at night and he never told me to scale back. I didn't feel I was allowed to work less. If I stopped taking on the extra work, it would continue to pile up and affect my work performance. What if my boss wrote me up? Or even worse, what if he fired me?

I needed the job and the money. I had zero savings and a heavy debt load. I didn't have a safety net. My immigrant parents couldn't bail me out if I lost my job. I didn't even have the option to move back home! My mom lived in an already overcrowded apartment, and my dad lived two and a half hours away in México.

Here I was, thinking I was Miss Independent because I had my own apartment and paid bills on time, but I was so *dependent* on my paycheck that I couldn't prioritize my well-being. I didn't have a way out. I had to deal with it just a little longer until we found a replacement.

The Breaking Point

Only the replacement didn't come soon enough. I kept running on fumes for another month, and eventually, my nervous system gave out on me.

It happened when I went to my doctor to get a refill on my Xanax prescription. I spent forty-five minutes in the waiting room sobbing and hyperventilating uncontrollably. I must have gone through twenty tissues to wipe all the tears and snot from my tormented face. The other patients in the waiting room stared at me and offered a sympathetic gaze. I slumped over defeatedly in my lobby room chair as I realized the superwoman who thought she could handle it all had broken. I felt like a failure and felt like a shell of myself.

When I finally went into the consultation room with my doctor, he asked me what was wrong. I told him all about my awful work situation. You know how doctor visits are usually short and rushed? Dr. Chong spent thirty minutes listening to me vent, and with compassion, he advised me never to risk my health over a job. I'll never forget it, and I still treasure it today.

I told him I knew I had reached my breaking point but couldn't stop working because I needed the job and the money. He told me not to worry and that he had a solution. He wrote me a doctor's note to get me mandatory time off work so that I'd have time to rest and heal. With this note, my job and source of income would be protected.

I breathed in a deep sigh of relief. I had finally gotten the break I desperately needed. I emailed the note to HR and took three weeks off to prioritize my physical and emotional well-being.

A New POV on Hustle Culture

After this awful burnout experience, I vowed never to let my work life interfere with my health again. Now, I act my wage.

We have extra work? Too bad, my shift ends at 5 p.m. I'll get to it the next day when I start my workday. And while you're at it, hire more people to pick up the extra slack. You're overdue on a deadline and need my help? Sorry! I have a Zumba class at 6 p.m. and won't be available. Sending you thoughts and prayers, though!

Now I know that understaffing is not an employee's problem. It's a business problem. So unless I'm an owner of the company, you aren't getting more than my regular work hours out of me. Now, of course, I'm diplomatic and professional in the way I deliver these boundaries. I'm not stupid. And I also put in a little extra time when absolutely necessary to get a project to the finish line. But now I know my limits, and as soon as I start feeling that I'm overworking and it's affecting my health, I prioritize me.

It took me living through this nightmare experience for me to know better, but what also helps is that I'm empowered by having an emergency fund that allows me to say "no" to a boss and say "yes" to me.

What is an emergency fund?

An emergency fund is a stash of cash set aside in case of a rainy day. Rainy days are bound to happen. They say two things are guaranteed in life: death and taxes. I'd add rainy days to that list.

Life isn't all rainbows and unicorns, although it should be! Rainy days are going to be hard, and they're going to be stressful. And unfortunately, a lot of people aren't financially prepared to weather the storm. According to Bankrate, 56 percent of Americans are unable to cover an unexpected $1,000 bill.[1] An emergency fund can help make most stressful life situations easier to navigate.

1   Reinicke, Carmen. "56% of Americans Can't Cover a $1,000 Emergency Expense with Savings." CNBC, January 19, 2022. https://www.cnbc.com/2022/01/19/56percent-of-americans-cant-cover-a-1000-emergency-expense-with-savings.html.

What do emergency funds do?

Emergency funds can be used when the unexpected happens, like if you crash your car and have to pay your $1,000 insurance deductible. Or if your appendix bursts and you need thousands of dollars to pay for the expensive ambulance ride. An emergency fund can be used to protect you if you get laid off from work or are suddenly fired and lose your main source of income. By having an emergency fund available to you, you can avoid getting into debt and worsening your financial situation. When life knocks you down toward the pavement face first, an emergency fund is the safety net that catches you.

An emergency fund also gives you the freedom to exit spaces that no longer serve you. If I'd had a healthy emergency fund, I would have felt financially secure enough to draw the line with my incompetent boss sooner. If he would have fired me, it wouldn't have been the end of the world. My emergency fund would have covered my basic life needs while I was job-searching for a new role. Instead of scrambling to find a new job and desperately accepting the first offer that came my way, it could have given me the space to take my time and find a workplace that truly aligned with my career goals and desired work-life balance. I could have left on my terms instead of working myself to exhaustion.

An emergency fund gives you the freedom to leave a bad roommate, an abusive partner, or a toxic workplace. But it's worth noting that emergency funds don't always have to be tied to life's tragedies. They can also give you a cash cushion to take an exciting career-elevating opportunity out of state if your new role doesn't cover your relocation costs. The morale of the story is: An emergency fund gives you options.

Why First Gen Need Emergency Funds

Emergency funds are nonnegotiable in our financial journey. It's why they're the first money topic we're covering as part of the First Gen Five. When life's worst happens, Privileged Pattys can have their parents bankroll their life while they ring up their old college buddies to set up a job interview for them. Average Amys can ask their reluctant parents for an interest-free loan while they get back on their feet.

As First-Gen, there is no safety net. None. When we fall, we fall hard, and it hurts like a MF. Which means we have to do the work to create that safety net for ourselves.

Limiting Beliefs about Emergency Funds

As I look back at some of the financial hardships that I've lived through in my twenties, I recognize a lot of them could have been avoided if only I'd had an emergency fund. Why hadn't I prioritized this sooner? ¡Que mensa!

Well, first, I'd never been taught about money, so I didn't even know I was supposed to have one. I also didn't understand the true benefits and how having one would make me feel safe. I had to live through turbulent times to recognize the value of an emergency fund. I try to show twenty-six-year-old me compassion for not knowing what I didn't know.

Here are some limiting beliefs that kept me from prioritizing savings as a young adult. As you read through them, notice if you resonate with any.

NOT FEELING WORTHY OF HAVING ONE

When I started hearing about the importance of having savings, I didn't feel savings was something that I was worthy of having.

Growing up in an immigrant household, the money situation at home had always been chaotic. My parents never had savings. If they ever needed extra money for an unexpected expense, they'd go to trusted friends or family for a small loan. That was my normal. Having a savings fund wasn't something I ever saw modeled at home, so having one felt more like a luxury than a necessity. It felt like savings were for people who had extra money to put away, not for people barely scraping by.

As a young adult, I was hardly getting by with my entry-level salary and didn't think I had a lot of extra money to put toward savings. Having an emergency fund felt like an overwhelming and unattainable goal. Because it felt so out of my reach, I didn't even bother trying.

Looking back, I now see I could have found an extra $20 a week to use toward savings. Although I was living paycheck to paycheck, I still managed to go out to brunch with friends or buy a new pair of yoga pants. I had a little money—I just didn't have the confidence that I could do it. I didn't understand that having *some savings* was better than having *no savings*. Building savings will help you feel financially secure.

THE NEGATIVE CONNOTATION OF "EMERGENCY"

For a long time, the word "emergency" triggered me. When I think of an emergency, I feel overwhelmed, chaotic, and uncertain. It doesn't feel good or empowering to think about what could go wrong in life. For years, I didn't prioritize saving for an emergency fund because it didn't feel good to save for something out of fear and negative emotions.

Luckily there's an easy fix for this. Give it a name that makes you feel safe and excited to save for it. If sassy and humorous is more your thing, that works too! Saving for an emergency fund should feel freeing and like you're prioritizing you. It's an act of self-care. This money isn't to pay off old debt or for a future you in forty years. It's for present you.

Here are some naming variations you can try:

- My safety net
- My peace of mind fund
- My saying yes to me fund
- My looking out for #1 fund
- Use in case of rainy days fund
- Murphy's Law fund
- When sh*t happens fund
- F U fund
- F**k white supremacy and the patriarchy fund

Pick a name that speaks to you, and just go with it. For the remainder of this chapter, I'll be referring to it as a peace of mind fund.

THINKING PAYING MY DEBT FIRST WAS MORE IMPORTANT

Another reason why I never prioritized building my peace of mind fund was because I owed debt. I had student loans that would take ten years to pay off and a five-figure car loan. At the time, I thought paying off my debt and becoming debt free was more important than creating savings. After all, wasn't I paying interest (or something like that) on this debt? I'll think about saving money once all my debt is paid off, I mistakenly thought.

Paying off debt is important and is also a part of the First Gen Five pillars. It's why we have an entire chapter dedicated to it later in this book. But by not having any savings put aside, I was risking getting into *more* debt if something unexpected came up.

The cash in your peace of mind fund is there to help you avoid taking on more debt, whether it's through a loan or a credit card. You can pay down debt from the past while also building savings for the future. You don't have to pick one or the other.

PLANNING TO USE MY CREDIT CARD AS MY PEACE OF MIND FUND

I thought that if I did have a financial emergency, I could use my credit card to cover the gap. Credit card debt is the worst kind of debt you can have, so planning to use your credit card for an emergency is not the savviest financial plan. Credit card debt can be very hard to pay off because of the high-interest charges (more on that later). On top of that, you can't pay for all your expenses with a credit card. If you get laid off from your job and don't have any savings, a lot of landlords won't let you use a credit card to pay for rent. You need extra cash set aside, even if it's just $500 to start out.

How much do you need in your peace of mind fund?

Now that you understand the full benefits of having a peace of mind fund and learned some of the common limiting beliefs that keep you from building one, you may be wondering, how much do you actually need?

Most financial experts recommend you save at least three to six months of your *monthly, bare minimum living expenses* to have a strong peace of mind fund. Your monthly bare minimum living expenses are the bare-bones cost of doing life. They are what it costs you to cover your basic necessities on a monthly basis. It includes essentials like the cost of housing, utilities, food, health insurance, and the minimum payments on debt you owe. It would not include any extras like the cost of eating out, salon visits, gifts, or vacations. This is just the bare minimum you need to survive.

Let's say you've added up all your monthly bare minimum living expenses, and they total up to $2,000. That means that to have a three- to six-month peace of mind fund, you'd need between $6,000–$12,000. According to Bankrate, 88 percent of people need enough to cover at least three months of their expenses for them to feel comfortable with their emergency savings.[2]

I know. It's a lot of money! A strong peace of mind fund could take months to build, possibly even years. And that's okay! It's not

---

2   Gillespie, Lane. "Bankrate's 2023 annual emergency savings report." Bankrate. June 22, 2023. https://www.bankrate.com/banking/savings/emergency-savings-report/

going to happen overnight. Mine took me almost two years to build. But the security you feel and the financial confidence you gain after reaching this big goal is 100 percent worth it.

How aggressive should you be with your peace of mind fund?

HOW STABLE IS YOUR JOB?

How much you should save depends on two factors: your job stability and how safe you want to feel. As I write, the tech industry is experiencing massive layoffs. According to Layoffs.fyi, over 160,000 tech employees were laid off in 2022.[3] Not long ago, everyone and their mama wanted to work in tech. They were drawn to the cushy $100,000+ salaries and lusted for employee perks like free massages and free on-site cafeterias. But if you work in tech in this current environment, you'll need a larger peace of mind fund than someone with a more stable and recession-proof job, like a nurse or a firefighter.

HOW SAFE DO YOU NEED TO FEEL?

It also depends on what makes you sleep better at night. Would you feel comfortable knowing you only have a three-month peace of mind fund available to you? Or would you feel safer if you had the full six months? After experiencing the pandemic and work disruptions, a lot of people feel safer having closer to twelve months'

3   Layoffs. https://layoffs.fyi/.

worth. I even know some people who have a two-year peace of mind fund. It all depends on what feels safe to you.

But beware: there is such a thing as having too much money set aside in case of an emergency. I had a money-coaching client who had $200,000 in cash socked away. That's too much in relation to what she truly needs to cover her minimum living expenses.

Once you've built enough savings to fully cover your peace of mind fund, any money in excess of that should be invested and positioned to grow (excluding any other short-term savings, like money you plan to use for a down payment or wedding costs in the near future). More about that in the investing chapter later in this book.

FYI: People who have experienced extreme poverty and hardship tend to hoard excess cash as a trauma response. If you have signs of financial trauma, please seek guidance from a mental health therapist who can help you rebuild a healthy relationship with money. Visit latinxtherapy.com or cliniciansofcolor.org to find a therapist near you.

ACTIVITY: WHAT'S YOUR PEACE OF MIND FUND GOAL?

Now take a moment and follow these steps to calculate your peace of mind fund goal:

1. Calculate your monthly bare minimum living expenses.

2. Multiply your answer by three. This amount is considered a skinny peace of mind fund.

3. Multiply your original answer from question 1 by six. This amount is considered a strong peace of mind fund.

4. Reflect: How stable is your job or industry? Is there a lot of employee turnover in your department? Is your role recession-proof? Do you have in-demand job skills that make you an attractive employee? Does having three months of savings set aside make you feel safe? Or would you feel safer having closer to six months? What about somewhere in between? There is no right or wrong answer, as every person has their own unique needs.

5. Set a peace of mind fund goal and get ready to tackle it!

How do you save that much money?

Now that you've decided how much you need in your peace of mind fund based on your monthly living expenses, your job stability, and how safe you want to feel, let's come up with a plan to meet your goal!

Using the previous example, let's pretend you decided on a three-month peace of mind fund of $6,000.

1. **Create microgoals:** Let's say you'd like to save $6,000 within the next two years. That can feel intimidating! It's a long time span and a big chunk of money. But what if you break

up the $6,000 into smaller, more digestible chunks? When you spread the $6,000 over twenty-four months, that evens out to $250/month. Saving $250 every month feels more doable. That is your micro goal, to save $250 every month until you reach your big goal. By setting microgoals, you're giving yourself more frequent opportunities to celebrate your financial wins, which will boost your confidence and keep you motivated to meet your big goal.

2. **Trim spending and set up an automatic transfer:** Now that you've set your micro goal of $250 a month, how do you come up with the money? Review your spending and trim out any unnecessary expenses you have, like unnecessary streaming services or extra dinner outings. The truth is that you have to get lean with your spending to create room for savings. It won't be forever. It's just while you're in savings mode. I promise! After completing this exercise, evaluate whether you have the space to save the $250 a month. If you do, ¡eso! Now set up an automatic transfer to have that money moved to your savings account. It beats doing it manually because, let's be real, you'll probably forget to do it, or even worse, you might spend it. Automating the transfer helps you build up your peace of mind fund on autopilot.

3. **Sell things you don't need:** But what if you cut all your spending and you still don't have the $250 available? Consider selling items you no longer use. Do you have any extra stuff collecting dust in your closet that you could sell? Maybe a guitar you haven't used in years or an old Peloton bike you use as a clothes rack? List your items on websites like OfferUp, Facebook marketplace, Craigslist, or Poshmark to sell your items online and get some quick cash. This quick

cash infusion can be used to jump-start your savings and encourage you to keep saving more.

4. **Make smart use of your windfalls:** A financial windfall is when you receive a large, often unexpected, amount of money. It can include cash that you don't receive regularly, like a bonus at work or a tax refund. Be intentional with this extra cash. Use a small portion of it (I like to use 20 percent) toward guilt-free and fun spending, like a nice massage or a fun night out with friends. But use the other 80 percent to make a big dent in your savings goal.

   Bonus tip: If you get paid biweekly by your employer, two months out of the year, you'll receive a third check. Map out when these extra checks will happen and use the same strategy, 20 percent for fun and 80 percent toward your peace of mind fund and watch your savings start to pile up!

5. **Pick up a side gig:** I'm not a fan of hustle culture or boss babe energy. I'm not going to tell you to work 24/7 to build this peace of mind fund. I don't think it's sustainable. Self-care and rest are necessary. Your physical and mental well-being is just as important as your financial well-being. But with the gig economy, it's easier than ever to make a quick buck on your terms. And when you make more, you can save more.

Back in my day, if you wanted to make some extra cash, you had to drag yourself to work somewhere like Jack in the Box. You'd put on a goofy uniform and wear ugly rubbery shoes, deal with a crappy, power-tripping boss, and get stuck working weekends because nobody else wanted to. With the gig economy, you have a lot more options now. According to Mastercard, the gig economy is expected to be valued at \$455 billion by 2023[4], which means the opportunities are almost limitless!

The flexibility you can get with gig work is unreal. You can set your own schedule, be your own boss, choose your clients, and set your own rate—sometimes while working in your pj's at home. You can sign up to be a pet sitter on Rover or help run errands for someone on Task Rabbit. If you'd rather make money from home, you can get paid to edit videos on Fiverr or be a virtual assistant in the creator economy. There are lots of ways to make money online. Check out websites like Fiverr, Freelancer.com, and Upwork to see what works best for you and start turbocharging your income!

The Best Place to Store Your Peace of Mind Fund

So far, we've covered how peace of mind funds protect you from the unexpected and give you the financial security to prioritize your well-being. We explored some of the most common limiting beliefs that can keep you from meeting your savings goals. We also discussed how to calculate how much money you should have in your peace of mind fund. Lastly, we went over actionable strategies you can use to create extra money to build savings. Now let's spend some time covering where you should keep your peace of mind fund.

To make real progress toward your savings goal, you'll need to set up a separate account to store your savings. If you keep your peace of mind fund in the same checking account you use to pay your everyday bills, it'll be harder to track your savings progress

4   "44 Eye-Opening Gig Economy Statistics for 2022." Velocity Global. https://velocityglobal.com/resources/blog/gig-economy-statistics/.

because your *spending money* will be mixed with your *savings money*. If your money is combined together, it'll also be easier to spend. You'll essentially be running in place and won't make any progress. The goal here is to save more, not to spend more.

A HIGH-YIELD SAVINGS ACCOUNT (HYSA) KEEPS YOUR MONEY SAFE

The best place to store your savings is in a **HYSA**. Most savings accounts will pay you very little interest (if any!) for holding your money at the bank. But that's not the case with a high-yield savings account. A high-yield savings account is a savings account that pays you a better rate than the national average. Your money is not locked up, and you have access to it at any time, the same way that you have access to your checking account money whenever you want. Many banks don't require a minimum balance to start, which means you can open a HYSA with as little as $10! It varies by bank.

A common misconception is that a high-yield savings account is an investment, but the reality is that it has nothing to do with the stock market. Your money is not being invested. It's just in a fancier savings account.

In simpler terms, a HYSA is just a *bougier savings account* that pays better than a dusty ol' savings account.

Think of it this way. If you've worked in the restaurant business you'll get this analogy. Imagine your regular savings account as that crappy tipper who left a $3 tip on a $100 restaurant tab. Nobody likes a crappy tipper! On the other hand, a high-yield account (the HYSA) acts like the better tipper that leaves you a respectable 25 percent tip you can feel excited about. Everybody prefers a bigger tip!

HOW MUCH MORE DOES A HYSA EARN?

According to Bankrate, the February 2023 national average yield for a regular savings account is 0.25 percent Annual Percentage Yield (APY).[5] As of this writing, my high-yield savings (HYSA) account at Ally Bank pays me 3.40 percent APY. That's almost fifteen times as much!

And this translates to real money. For example, let's say you have $10,000 stored in a high-yield savings account. With a 3.40 percent APY, a savings balance of $10,000 would earn a little over $300 after a year. Those same $10,000 would only get you about $20 in a regular savings account. Like I said, crappy tipper.

Are you going to retire off $300? Absolutely not. But why not get paid $25 a month to store your money instead of $1.66? That's a monthly Chipotle burrito *with* guac, chips, and a drink—all on the bank's dime. Yes, please!

HOW TO AVOID SPENDING YOUR PEACE OF MIND FUND

Now that I got you all excited about high-yield savings accounts, my next hot tip is to open this HYSA at a **different bank** than where you have your checking account.

Let's say you have your checking account at Chase. If you had your checking and HYSA at Chase, you could easily transfer money back and forth between the two accounts at any moment. The money transfer would be instant. If you overspent a little this month, no worries. You can transfer a little money from your HYSA to your checking account to cover all your bills.

And the same thing the next month. And the month after that.

5   Goldberg, Matthew. "What Is the Average Interest Rate for Savings Accounts?" Bankrate, June 22, 2023. https://www.bankrate.com/banking/savings/average-savings-interest-rates/.

And so on. This bad habit can be difficult to break, and it's not going to help you build savings! Trust me, I've danced that dance too.

Instead of opening a HYSA with your checking account bank, open it at a completely different bank. Opening a new account at a different bank will require a little more legwork, but it will also make it harder for you to spend the money since you won't have easy access to it anymore. Transferring money between two banks takes a couple of days, which will act as a barrier and help prevent frequent transfers. Online banks tend to give you the best HYSA rates since they don't have physical buildings to maintain as brick-and-mortar banks do. You can also check your local credit unions for a competitive rate.

If you want to know my favorite high-yield savings accounts, including the HYSAs with the biggest sign-on bonuses and highest-paying APY, visit culturaandcash.com to download the C&C Resource Pack and access an up-to-date list.

Peace of Mind Funds for the Familia

So what about when your family needs help with an emergency? Use the Quiero y Puedo approach to guide you in your decision-making process. Remember, your peace of mind fund is *your* safety net to use when life gets rough. If it's a true emergency, like helping your family pay rent to avoid eviction, then you may need to tap into your peace of mind fund. But make sure to replenish that money ASAP because the point of a peace of mind fund is to have money available to *you* when *you* need it.

FAMILY PEACE OF MIND FUND

If you've decided you want to help family with unexpected expenses, you can create a family peace of mind fund. This would be money set apart from your personal savings, so open a second savings account to keep the money separate.

My partner and I are doing something like this for our aging parents. As they get older, they'll need more money to cover medical costs. It's important for us to have the ability to help if needed, so we each add $50 a month to a savings account just for our parents. Our goal is to build the account to $5,000. It won't happen overnight; it will take years to build. But with this plan, we'll have a way to support our family when they need it most without derailing our budget, getting us into debt, or dipping into our personal peace of mind fund. Win, win, and win!

SETTING BOUNDARIES WITH PEACE OF MIND FUNDS

What if you tried the Quiero y Puedo approach and decided you don't have the willingness or financial means to help with an unexpected cost? If that's the case, plan to have a transparent and loving conversation with your family.

A few years ago, my grandma needed eye surgery. My tía in México called me and asked me to pitch in $1,000 to help with the surgery costs. She assumed that because I worked in "el otro lado," I'd readily have the money available. I didn't. I wanted to help, but I couldn't afford to, and to be honest, $1,000 is a big ask.

Culturally insensitive advice says "no" is a complete sentence. That doesn't work with Latine families. We need more care and compassion for our families. This is what financial boundaries could look like for us:

- **Scenario 1:** "I'm sorry to hear about Grandma. I want to help, but money is tight right now. I can't give the $1,000, but I can give $250. What's the easiest way to transfer you the money?"

- **Scenario 2:** "I'm sorry to hear about Grandma. I want to help, but money is tight right now. I can't give the $1,000. I can loan you $400, but I need it to be paid back. Would you be okay with this arrangement?"

- **Scenario 3:** "I'm sorry to hear about Grandma. I want to help, but money is tight right now. Are there other ways I can support you through this time of need? I can buy groceries for the week and cook while she recovers if that helps."

- **Scenario 4:** "I'm sorry to hear about Grandma. I want to help, but I won't be able to swing it. I hope you understand. I'll be thinking of her and will make sure to visit her at the hospital after her surgery."

The idea is to offer the type of support you're willing and able to give. It should be an arrangement you feel comfortable with. You can use these same prompts to set financial boundaries when a loved one asks you for a monthly allowance, asks you to loan them money, or asks to use your credit. We'll explore this further in upcoming chapters.

Financial Security Starts with a Peace of Mind Fund

The reason I'm such a big proponent of people starting their financial journey with a strong focus on a peace of mind fund is that I could have avoided one of the darkest times in my life had I had one. Even if I'd had a skinny peace of mind fund that could have floated me for three months, I would have been able to tell my exploitative boss to kick rocks sooner. I could have prioritized my mental health.

I could have preserved my peace of mind. But I didn't because I didn't have one. I don't want this to happen to you.

Having savings gives you the freedom to do what's best for you. You've worked too hard to be at someone else's mercy. A peace of mind fund gives you that control back. Remember, *you deserve to be free of financial worries.*

Reaching your savings goal will take time, commitment, and patience. But once you've reached your goal, you'll feel more secure and confident in your ability to make good financial moves, which leads to more positive money behavior.

To meet this big financial milestone, you'll need to learn strong budgeting skills. A budget will help you become aware of where you're spending your money and will show you the areas you can cut back on to meet your goal faster.

In the next chapter, we'll talk about how a spending plan can bring you clarity and act as a road map to help you reach competing financial goals. See you there!

CHAPTER 4

BUDGETING IS YOUR BFF

I have the power to create success and build the wealth I desire.

One by one, I scanned the sea of photos on the classroom wall looking for a familiar face. The photo collage I was eyeing had pictures of former high school students from the late '90s and early 2000s. And then I spotted my seventeen-year-old self. There I was, in my purple and gold cap and gown, beaming with pride at my high school graduation. That day I was back in my hometown of El Centro, CA, to speak at my former high school's career day.

El Centro is a small, agricultural border town about thirty minutes north of the border near Baja California, México. Well-paying careers in El Centro were only for the privileged few. Anybody from the area knew that if you wanted to "make good money," you either had to work in the nursing sector, US Customs, or US Border Patrol. Or, if you were lucky, you had a palanca that could hook you up with a cushy county job. Most of the other jobs in the area were low-paying jobs in retail or hospitality.

This is why my dad jokingly calls it "El Valle de la Muerte." As someone who grew up there, I knew I could make an impact if I attended career day and exposed high school students to other jobs outside of those sectors. I got in touch with my favorite high school teacher (shoutout to Mr. J!) and asked him if he needed a speaker for the annual event.

I spoke to six classrooms of Algebra II students and told them about my career journey to investment management. I talked to them about how I navigated community college, how I left our cow town and transferred to UCSB, why I picked econ as my major, and how I started my career in finance. Surprisingly, the teenage students clung to every word of my story and asked thoughtful questions during the Q and A portion. I told them all the highs and lows of my corporate career and shared my biggest college regret: not studying abroad.

I didn't study abroad because I couldn't afford it. Back then, I was paying for all my college expenses with student loans, and I didn't want to take out more loans for a carefree semester abroad. I was also nervous about my job prospects once I graduated. I didn't have connections or parents with a professional network that could open any doors for me. With all the uncertainty, the last thing I needed was to burden myself with an additional $10,000 to my college debt just to sip sangria and eat tapas abroad in Spain for a semester.

I figured Barcelona would still be there later once I graduated and had a big-girl salary. *Why travel as a broke college student when I can go as a bougie corporate baddie?*

What I didn't realize is that, yes, although I'd have more money as a full-time employee, I would have much less *time* to travel. I told the kids that when you work in corporate, you're lucky to get a two- to three-week vacation a year—if that! I urged them to study abroad, even if it meant taking out loans. I explained studying abroad was a rare chance to live in a foreign country and experience a new culture for two to three months while still young and with little to no adult responsibilities. I told them I knew a lot of friends who took on debt to study abroad, and not a single one of them regretted it. If anything, their faces still lit up with joy when they relived their study abroad experience. The only people who regretted it were the people who didn't go. People like me.

After leaving career day, I reflected on my day and my big regret of not studying abroad. Well, at least I warned the kids and helped them avoid the same mistake I did. But what about me? Is that it? Did I completely miss the boat on my travel dreams?

These questions were the starting point of one of the most profound principles of First Gen Five: a budget. Or as I like to call it, a spending plan.

How My Dream to Travel Led to Budgeting

Speaking to the kids in my hometown sparked a new fire in me to consider how I could make my travel dreams a reality. I knew a lot of people typically traveled in their sixties post-retirement, but the thought of postponing my travel dreams until retirement brought me more horror than comfort. *Thirty whole-ass years?! I'm supposed to wait thirty-plus years to travel? What if I don't make it? What if I die young and beautiful like Marilyn Monroe? What if I make it to my sixties but have a bad knee like my grandma? What if I have unbearable back pain like my uncle? How am I supposed to climb up historic towers in Europe with an achy body?* Waiting until I retire in my sixties can't be the only way.

Like any desperate person looking for an answer, I ran to the internet to Google "*How . . . do . . . I . . . travel . . . while . . . I'm . . . young?*" I typed frantically on my phone. Most of the search results were articles on studying abroad or teaching English in a foreign country. Yeah, not helpful. I had no aspirations to go back to school for a master's, and I knew I wouldn't be able to finance my lifestyle with a measly ESL teacher salary. As I scrolled further down the results page, I came across an article about sabbaticals.

A sabbatical is an extended period of rest or break away from work. Sabbaticals are commonplace in academia. Tenured university professors take one-year breaks away from work every seven years to travel, study—or do both. But I learned you didn't have to be a professor to take a sabbatical. Anyone could take a sabbatical from work, but you either had to have your employer pay for it or fund it yourself.

This could work! Maybe I wouldn't have to wait until retirement to travel long-term. As I read more articles on sabbaticals, I learned that a lot of people referred to them as "midcareer breaks." After reviewing the employee handbook, I found my cheap-ass employer didn't offer paid sabbaticals. I also learned that the few companies that did offer them usually required you to work there for five to ten years before qualifying for one. I didn't want to wait that long. This meant that if I wanted to take a career break, I had to pay for it myself.

From my online research, I found most people could take a 'round-the-world trip and quit their job for a year for $25,000 to $30,000 dollars. ¡No manches! That's a lot of money. After paying rent, my student loans, my car payment, groceries, and all else, I had little left at the end of the month. I really wanted to take a sabbatical, but how am I supposed to fund such a big goal?

According to others who'd taken sabbaticals, I found there were typically three ways people paid for this:

1. They'd get laid off and use their severance pay.

2. They'd receive an inheritance from their family.

3. They budgeted and saved up the money.

So I could get laid off and hope to receive severance pay? Hmm, it didn't sound like the smartest strategy. Who wants to get laid off, after all?

As a First-Gen, I didn't have a rich aunt about to croak and leave me all her fortune, so option #2 was out of the equation. Which meant I was only left with option #3—budgeting.

I was determined to make this dream happen. From reading others' experiences, budgeting could be the solution to make my dream come true! But I didn't know the first thing about budgeting. I'd never been taught it at school or at home.

I was committed to learning everything I could about budgeting. I read all the personal finance books I could get a hold of and binge-listened to money podcasts. I made a series of smart money moves, like moving to a lower-cost-of-living area, and really mastered intentional spending. I bought a huge world map from Amazon to keep me motivated and used pushpins to label cities I wanted to visit on my 'round-the-world trip. I daydreamed out loud with my partner, and we'd share the activities and sights we'd see abroad. I tracked and understood where my money went every month. I had it down to a science. Budgeting didn't feel like a chore. It felt like an exciting game I got to practice every month that brought me closer and closer to my big dream.

Within two and a half years, I paid off all my debt and saved $20,000—I was more than two-thirds of the way to my $30,000 goal to quit my job and travel the world. What once felt like an impossible goal was now a close reality. I was on my way to achieving my dream of traveling thanks to the power of budgeting.

Spoiler alert: I never did get to go on that round-the-world trip. Thanks to the COVID-19 pandemic in 2020, all travel plans came to a screeching halt. My travel sabbatical would have to come at a later date. But that money sure came in handy when I quit my full-time job in 2021 to pursue a new career as a creative entrepreneur. And I feel confident that this new career will one day offer me the flexibility to travel on my terms. The lesson here is budgeting and learning to be intentional with my money gave me *options*. And I want the same for you!

What is a budget?

There's a popular phrase in the personal finance community: "If you don't tell your money where it needs to go, you'll be wondering where it went." A budget helps you keep track of where your money is going every month so you can make sure your money is working for you and helping you reach your life goals. Your budget works as a road map to help you get to where you want to go.

Would you drive to a new address without using GPS? No, right? You'd enter the destination on your phone and map out how to get there. A budget provides that same level of direction for your money and life goals.

A budget helps you pay your bills on time, avoid debt, pay down existing debt, and save and invest for future financial goals. When done right, budgeting can be extremely liberating. Instead of ignoring your spending, you'll feel confident in having a clear picture of where your money is going every month. A healthy budget will help you execute the rest of the pillars in the First Gen Five, including building a peace of mind fund.

Budgeting Myths and Truths

When I teach budgeting at a live financial literacy workshop, I always like to start the conversation by explaining what budgeting *is not*. Budgeting gets such a bad rap! I blame our consumerist and capitalist society for this. They bombard us with messages to "buy, buy, buy!" even though it may not be what we need at the moment. Budgeting is almost used as a dirty word. For example, saying something is "low budget" or saying "I'm on a budget" automatically has a negative connotation and means you're a broke bitch. This is very far from the truth. More about this in a bit.

My goal in this section is to help you view budgeting not as something you should begrudgingly do but as an exciting tool and road map to help you achieve your life goals and dreams. By the end of this chapter, you'll be equipped with the first steps you need to take to start your new relationship with budgeting.

MYTH: IF YOU'RE ON A BUDGET, YOU'RE A BROKE BITCH

Truth: If you're on a budget, you're a responsible bitch with goals. *And since when is it a bad thing to have goals?*

When I was in my early twenties, I was always the broke one in my friend group. My friends were either in higher-paying industries or shared living expenses with their partners, and they had more disposable income. My job paid me $45,000 a year, and I lived on my own, which doesn't go very far in a big city like Los Angeles.

On the weekends, we enjoyed going out to brunch at expensive and trendy restaurants. I couldn't afford these outings like they could. And I didn't feel comfortable saying I couldn't afford it. So what did I do instead? I charged the tab to my credit card. Over and over again. Socializing at a bottomless mimosa Sunday brunch with my friends was fun and glamorous, but you know what wasn't? Getting myself into four figures of credit card debt.

Now I understand that being on a budget means you have clear financial goals and a spending plan to reach them. And that's something you should be proud of!

The language you use matters. Instead of saying, "I can't afford that," try saying, "That's not a priority for me right now," or "I don't value that enough to pay for it." It's a way to claim your power back and show that a budget is not something that's happening to you—it's something you're intentionally executing because you have bigger plans with your money. And we love to see an empowered woman running the show!

MYTH: THERE'S NO POINT IN BUDGETING IF YOU'RE LIVING PAYCHECK TO PAYCHECK

Truth: If you have lesser means, it's even more crucial for you to have a budget.

This one is common for a lot of children of immigrants. Most of us grew up in a low-income family and lived paycheck to paycheck, so it's hard for us to feel we can live beyond what we saw growing up. This is rooted in the scarcity mindset we talked about in Chapter 2. There isn't much room to daydream about *getting ahead* when you're hardly *getting by*.

But I'm here to tell you that you can be the first in your family to break the paycheck-to-paycheck cycle! Our parents came to this country exactly for this reason. Your parents didn't leave everything they knew and loved behind for you to be scraping by and counting the days until your next direct deposit. They came here to give us and future generations the opportunity to live a better life.

As the first to graduate from college, you have a higher earning potential than they ever did and the financial means to get ahead. This is something that was never afforded to them with their minimum-wage jobs. I can't think of a better way to honor their sacrifice than to live a rich and fulfilling life on your terms.

I'd like to acknowledge that budgeting won't work for everyone. There are systemic issues that keep a lot of Black, Indigenous, and other people of color in poverty and in the paycheck-to-paycheck cycle. It's incredibly difficult to budget or manifest your way out of poverty when the system is rigged against you. As a First Gen college graduate, you hold more privilege than others before you and have the opportunity to escape the cycle of poverty. Use it and lead the way for others in your family to do the same.

Lastly, I know what it feels like to have little hope in budgeting when you have little left over at the end of the month. If you're earlier in your career, chances are you graduated with student debt and have a modest entry-level salary. When I graduated from college, I was lucky if I even had $100 to my name after rent, food, and the rest of my big-girl bills. You may feel budgeting is something that only makes sense for people who have the money for it. But I'd argue that budgeting is not just for the rich or those who have disposable income. If you're working with a smaller salary, it's even **more crucial** for you to have a clear picture of where your money is going at the end of the month. Rich people can afford to be reckless with their money—the rest of us can't.

MYTH: AS I GO UP THE CORPORATE LADDER, I'LL MAKE MORE MONEY AND WON'T NEED TO WORRY ABOUT A BUDGET

Truth: More money doesn't necessarily solve your money problems!

I used to believe that as I grew in my career, my income would increase, and my finances would magically fall into place. But the truth is, someone earning $500,000 a year can still be living paycheck to paycheck. If someone makes $500k but they spend $500k on an extravagant lifestyle, they're living paycheck to paycheck. These people are called HENRYs in the personal finance world: high earners, not rich yet.

Making more money is one part of the equation (a big part), but money doesn't go very far if you aren't strategic and have a plan for it.

If you don't have a plan for your money, you know who will? The multi-billion-dollar advertising industry. The advertising industry spends a lot of money and resources to understand human psychology and what causes our spending patterns. They weaponize this knowledge to trigger our emotional spending and get us to buy their products or services. They don't care about our budget or life goals. They just care about selling their product.

As an in-demand influencer, I know firsthand how much money these companies throw into advertising. My biggest sponsor to date paid me almost $20,000 for a single TikTok video. That's more than three times my monthly salary at my last corporate job! Fortunately, the companies I get sponsored by are typically in the money management space, and their products either help you make money or save money, not spend it. I'm not dragged into peddling excessive consumerism like other content creators, so my conscience is clear.

Back in the day, advertisers could only reach us if we listened to their commercial on the radio or saw their billboard on the highway. But now, they have access to us 24-7 through our cell phone and with digital marketing, which means it's more important than ever to create your own plan for your money. I don't know about you, but I care too much about my money to let white men in suits manipulate how I spend it.

Not having a spending plan also puts you at risk of falling into a trap called **lifestyle creep**. Lifestyle creep is when you spend more money on nonessentials because your income went up. For example, let's say you got a promotion at work and will now make an additional $20,000. Congrats! If you have debt or savings goals, the financially savvy thing to do would be to keep your current lifestyle and current spending the same and use the extra $20,000 toward getting out of debt or building up savings.

But that's not what most people do. Most people get a $20,000 raise and think, "F**k yeah! Now I can buy a new car and move into a luxury apartment building with the extra money I have. I deserve this." When their old car and apartment building were perfectly fine. This cycle can keep you running in place instead of advancing toward your financial goals.

MYTH: IF I'M ON A BUDGET, I CAN'T DO ANYTHING FUN. IT'S LIKE I'M BEING PUNISHED FOR NOT HAVING MORE MONEY.

Truth: A well-crafted budget doesn't feel like a chore because it's aligned with your unique goals and spending values.

If your budget feels like you're depriving yourself of the things you love, you're doing it wrong. A budget is very similar to a diet. If you're trying to get healthier and put yourself on a restrictive diet with nothing but lean chicken breast and leafy greens seven days a week, you'll be miserable. And you can't sustain something you are miserable doing. You won't be able to stick to it long enough to get real results. The trick is to pick a diet you can stick to, like a balanced diet with a majority of healthy meals, but that allows space for the occasional cheat meal or treat to reward yourself along the way. That is how you get results.

The same is true for a budget. If your budget is only used for "responsible things" and it doesn't give you space for spending on things that bring you joy, you'll lose motivation quickly, ditch your budget, and forget all about your goals.

Traditional personal finance experts (a.k.a. old, white Boomers) love to bully people for buying a daily iced coffee or splurging on avocado toast. But if those things genuinely bring you joy, you can find a way to keep them in your spending plan.

For me, I like to splurge on regular manicures and pedicures. Others may think they're a waste of money since you can do your nails at home for a fraction of the cost. But for me, a fresh gel manicure makes me feel pretty, feminine, and put together. It makes me feel confident and keeps me motivated to work toward my dreams. I consider it self-care. Spending $100+ a month at the nail salon is how I choose to spend my money intentionally. The key is to spend according to your values and goals instead of mindlessly spending on stuff that doesn't matter to you.

A healthy budget is the road map that helps you bring your financial dreams to life.

MYTH: BUDGETING IS DIFFICULT AND COMPLICATED, ESPECIALLY FOR SOMEONE LIKE ME WHO'S NEVER BEEN GOOD AT MATH!

Truth: You have the math skills you need to execute your own budget!

Do you know the answer to 2 + 2? Or 3 x 2? How about 10 ÷ 2? If you answered 4, 6, and 5, then guess what? You have what you need to budget. I know math can be a little intimidating if you don't consider it your forte, but you really only need to know some basic arithmetic to create and maintain your spending plan.

Some budgets can be more complex than others. We'll talk more about common budgeting methods later in this chapter. But your budget is only as complicated as you choose to make it. You don't need to be an Excel nerd or a differential calculus whiz to use a budget.

Quick Chapter Check-In

We covered quite a bit, so let's do a quick recap of what we've learned:

- A budget is a spending plan that can help bring your financial dreams to life.
- Think of a budget as a road map to accomplish your financial goals.
- Spending according to your budget shows you are in control—not society, not the advertisers, not your friend group or your family!
- The key to making a budget stick is crafting one that is based on your unique values and goals.
- Budgeting math is simple. You only need basic arithmetic skills.
- Budgeting is your BFF. Stop resisting it and embrace it. You won't regret it.

Lastly, I interviewed some close friends and colleagues, all First Gen professionals, for research for this book. Across the board, they all said one of their biggest financial regrets was **not budgeting sooner**. Nobody said they wished they'd done it later. Learn from their regrets and start embracing budgeting now.

Start with Your Why

By now, I hope I've helped you overcome the initial resistance you might have felt when you heard the B-word. Now that you understand budgeting is the foundation to achieve your financial dreams and goals let's talk about how you actually create a budget.

The first step to creating your spending plan is figuring out your why.

The power of why was best explained by Oprah during an appearance on *The Daily Show*. The host at the time, Trevor Noah, asked her, "You've talked to everyone in the world who is successful. What would you say is the one common characteristic that you find gets people where they want to go?"

Oprah answered, "People get to where they want to go because they *know where they want to go.*"

She goes on to explain that most people don't really know what they want out of life. They're driven by what they *think* they should do or what other people say they should do. But the most important question you can ask yourself is, "What do I really want?"

When your values and goals are clearly defined, it will be much easier to make consistent steps to get you toward your desired purpose. Your vision is what's going to motivate you to push forward when things get tough. Having clear goals can serve as a powerful anchor to keep you focused on what really matters to you and shift your spending habits from mindless spending to intentional spending.

This is actually my favorite part of the process! This is where we hold space to reflect on what our dream life looks like and what financial goals we need to achieve to get there. Like Kourtney Kardashian says, "We all have different priorities," so what you define as your dream life might be very different from the person next to you.

ACTIVITY: DARE TO DREAM!

Put some relaxing music on, cozy up on your couch with a warm cafecito, and ask yourself the questions below. Write down the answers in a journal. Don't judge yourself for your responses. Nobody else is seeing your responses besides you, so feel free to unleash and dream big. No dream is too big!

As much as you may be tempted, please don't skip this step. It's not busywork. I've found incredible momentum from journaling these types of questions and want this exercise to do the same for you.

continued

- If money weren't an issue, what would your dream life look like? How would you spend your mornings? How would you spend your evenings?

- Would you work? What type of work would you do? Would you work full-time, part-time, or seasonally? If you don't dream of labor, then how do you envision spending your time?

- What types of vacations do you want to go on? Relaxed and tropical? Adventurous and fast-paced?

- How much time would you spend with your immediate family? What about your extended family? Would you see them every day, a couple of times a month, or a couple of times a year?

- Where would you like to live? In a quiet home in the country? In a trendy condo in an urban city? Perhaps abroad experiencing a new culture?

- Is financially supporting family a priority for you? Do you want to buy your parents a house or help them retire? Do you want to set up your children to have an easier life than you did and pass on generational wealth to them?

- Would you spend any time volunteering? What social causes or grassroots organizations would you like to make an impact in, whether it's with your time or monetary donations?

- Do you have any aspirations to start your own business? What would your business be about? What would it sell, and who would it serve and impact? Why are you interested in this business?

- Do you want to retire earlier than the traditional age of sixty-five? Or report to a boss until you're old and gray?

- Are you a lifelong learner? Do you want to go to grad school and graduate debt free?

- Are you ready to set some roots and settle down in one place? Are you ready to have a home and decorate it however you want?

- What financial goals would you like to achieve in a year? What about in five years? And in ten? Twenty?

Getting this kind of clarity is what helped me pay off $20,000 of debt and save fourteen months of my living expenses in just two and a half years. For me, my why was a big dream to quit my job for a year so I could travel the world young. I wanted to experience new cultures and travel at my own pace without having to rush through a two-week vacation and then come back to a pile of work. This is a dream *I wanted*. Not a dream my parents or society wanted for me. My big dream kept me focused. It helped me pay down debt and save money when I was tempted by distractions that were going to derail my travel goals.

ACTIVITY: WRITE YOUR MONEY GOALS

Take some uninterrupted time to answer the previous questions thoughtfully. Write out what you'd like to accomplish financially in the next six months, one year, and five years.

Here are some examples to get you started: Pay off student debt, save for an emergency fund, save for a vacation, save for a new car, pay off credit card debt, save for a down payment, and save for wedding expenses.

Completing this exercise will be the first step in you getting clarity on what you really want to accomplish with your money. You need a vision to spend mindfully and in alignment with your life goals. Once your answers are complete, your next step will be to keep your goals in sight.

Keep Your Goals Visible

Did you know that only 9 percent of people keep their New Year's resolutions? A new year inspires many to look inward and set big life visions. They get really excited about the possibility of learning a skill, exercising more, or quitting smoking. But those hopes and dreams evaporate as early as February once the initial excitement wears off. My take: they lose their motivation because they lose sight of their goal.

Now that you've gotten clear on what lifestyle and financial goals are important to you make sure to keep these goals at the top of your mind always. Here are some different ways you can do that:

- **Create a vision board:** A vision board is a collage of pictures and quotes of all your dreams and desires. You can clip magazine images or print photos from the internet. You can also buy a vision board kit online for relatively cheap. Create a vision board that represents your wildest dreams. Keep your vision board somewhere visible, like your bedroom wall, to see it daily. Every time you see your vision board, it will motivate and inspire you to keep working toward your goals.

  - Pro tip: Get together with your amigas on a weekend evening and do a vino and vision boarding night!

- **Listen to podcasts:** I kept my dream of traveling the world alive by listening to travel podcasts. I binged podcast interviews with people who taught English abroad, took sabbaticals, or got a work assignment abroad. Hearing how others did it, as well as learning from their mistakes, was inspiring and helped keep me focused on my goal.

- **Watch TV shows:** Podcasts not your jam? Try watching TV shows for similar results. Let's say your dream is to buy your first home. Watch TV shows like *House Hunters* or *Fixer Upper* for inspo for your future home aesthetic!

- **Join communities:** There's a lot of power in finding community with a common goal, whether it's virtual or in person. This is especially helpful when those closest to you aren't as committed to their financial journey as you are. Instead of going at it alone, find your people. Call me a Boomer, but I still enjoy a good ol' Facebook group with like-minded women. The best

Facebook groups have ongoing discussions where people ask each other questions, seek advice, or share resources. You can also check out Discord communities and Slack channels. The C&C Resource Pack includes access to an exclusive Discord channel where you can meet and get support from other readers of this book. Access it at culturaandcash.com.

- **Read books:** Check out fiction or nonfiction books from your local library for some inspo! I read enlightening memoirs like *Eat, Pray, Love*; *Under the Tuscan Sun*; and practical how-to books on how to plan for a sabbatical to keep me motivated.

- **Use your phone lock screen:** According to Zippia, the average American checks their phone ninety-six times a day, or once every ten minutes.[1] Use this bad habit to your benefit. If one of your big goals is to vacation in Peru, try saving a photo of Machu Picchu as your phone lock screen to keep your dream vacation always visible. You can try doing this for your computer desktop background too.

- **Hire a money coach:** A money coach is the costliest of these options but one to consider if you'd benefit from some one-on-one accountability. A money coach is a financial expert who can guide you through the steps you need to achieve a desired goal. They can review your income and spending patterns to help you devise a customized spending plan tailored to your unique needs. A money coach provides accountability, support, and ongoing financial education to keep you on track and help you meet your goals.

---

1   Flynn, Jack. "20 Vital Smartphone Usage Statistics [2023]: Facts, Data, and Trends on Mobile Use in the US" Zippia: The Career Expert. April 3, 2023. https://www.zippia. com/advice/smartphone-usage-statistics/#:~:text=The%20average%20American%20 spends%205,or%20once%20every%20ten%20minutes.

Las Aparencias and Intentional Spending

So far, we've covered how budgeting is the foundation for reaching your financial goals. We talked about some of the most common budgeting myths that can keep you from starting your budgeting journey. We discussed how identifying your why and getting clear on your life vision can serve as a strong motivator to reach your financial goals. Lastly, we outlined actionable strategies you can use to keep your life vision present at all times and how this visual reminder can keep your dream alive.

Now let's spend some time talking about intentional spending and why it can feel a little foreign for the Latine community.

Practicing intentional spending plays a big factor in how successful you are with your budget. You can spend hours creating a detailed and elaborate budget, but if you're consistently overspending, you'll be left with little money to move the needle with your financial goals. Not only do we live in a capitalist society that's constantly bombarding us with messages to buy, but culturally we're also taught to care about "las aparencias."

In the Latine community, it's very common to feel we have to dress or live a certain way to get exterior validation and be viewed as successful. We give a lot of value to what people think about us. "If I wear these old rags, what will people say?" "If I drive an older car, ¿qué va a decir la gente?"

The popular Spanish phrase "Antes muerta que sencilla" comes to mind. It literally translates to "I'd rather be dead than plain." And when it's common for us to size each other up by what we wear or what we drive, we can easily fall into the overspending trap to try to portray something we are not. After all, as a community, we don't talk about money because it's taboo, right? We don't share our net worth, our outstanding debt, or our credit score. The only way we can evaluate how well our neighbor lives is by what is visible to the eye.

When you cave into the pressures of las aparencias, you are giving more importance to what others think than your own life goals.
Resist the pressure to people please, and get comfortable standing
strong in what's actually important to you. This won't always feel
easy, especially when we've been conditioned to seek our family's
and community's approval. But it is very necessary to see the change
we want to see in our finances.

BE CHEAP AND BE BOUGIE IN THE WAYS
YOU WANT TO BE

How do you change your mindset to one of an intentional spender?
Remember, intentional spending is when you spend money with
purpose. It's the opposite of impulsive spending. An intentional
spender spends money guilt-free on things they truly value and
cuts down unapologetically on what isn't important to them. It
feels empowering to spend money on what matters to you because
you're in the driver's seat. With intentional spending, you control
where your money goes. You no longer fall into pressures to spend
by advertisers or societal expectations.

I have a popular video series on TikTok called "3 Things I'm
Cheap With and 3 Things I'm Bougie With." One of the reasons the
series performs so well is that people have lots of opinions on what
is and isn't worthy of spending money on. I share that I'm extremely
cheap with furniture. I use cheap, college-dorm-room-style plastic
drawers from Target to store my clothes. I don't get joy or happiness
from having a nice piece of furniture to look at. Sorry, I just don't!

Some people feel a married woman in her thirties should have
a proper dresser in her home. That's fine. They can think whatever
they want. They're not paying my bills. But because I'm cheap with
furniture and many other things I don't care about, I'm able to be
bougie with the things I love.

I love spending money on concert tickets. One year I spent $1,000 to see Ariana Grande on the Sweetener World Tour. Some people would never dream of spending that much money on a concert ticket. But for me, there is no better feeling than belting to "7 Rings" from a front-row seat surrounded by fellow Arianators. I want it—I got it!

To practice intentional spending and avoid impulsive spending, try these strategies:

- **"Is this a want or a need?"**: This is something I still ask myself to this day! When shopping, whether online or in person, take a moment to pause and ask yourself: Is this a want or a need? Do I need this purchase right now? If it's a need, like groceries for the week, then spend guilt-free. If you answer honestly and admit it's a want, evaluate whether buying it is practicing intentional spending. This happens to me a lot when I buy clothes. When I find a great pair of shorts that makes my booty pop in all the right places, I impulsively want to buy one in every color. I'm just so happy to find something that looks good on me! But when I take a moment to pause and ask myself whether I *need* all five colors or I *want* all five colors, that moment of pause helps me make better buying decisions. I'll keep two pairs and put the other three back on the rack. It feels good to be in control and make intentional spending choices!

- **"Does spending on this get me closer or further from my goals?"**: If you answered, this is a want, that's okay! Money isn't only to be used for necessities. You also have to spend money on things and experiences that make you happy. As we discussed, being too restrictive with your spending will make you feel deprived and can lead to you ditching your budgeting plans. The trick is balancing the occasional splurges while still making progress toward your money goals.

- **Shop with a list:** Have you ever been to Target to buy some laundry detergent but ended up at the checkout line with a cart full of Target goodies? We've all been there. They call it the Target Effect. Retail stores are designed to trick us into spending more than we need. Why do you think they have a Starbucks in Target stores? They know that if you have a coffee to drink while shopping, you'll take your time perusing through the aisles, and the more time you spend at the store, the more likely you are to buy things you didn't really need. The same can happen when you go grocery shopping hungry. When you shop on an empty stomach, you become less thoughtful about what you should buy and more driven to satisfy your hunger by buying anything—at the expense of your grocery budget.

To avoid overspending, try writing out a shopping list before you leave your home, and make a verbal commitment to stick to it as best as you can. If it's not on the list, but you still want it, go back to our two previous questions.

Four Key Elements to Building a Budget

We've covered the money mindsets you'll need to adopt a budget successfully. Now let's talk about how to create a spending plan. This will take some time to sort out, so set aside one to two hours to sit down and compile all this information. If it's too much to get through in one sitting, try breaking it up into two sessions. You can track all the information on a spreadsheet or a notebook, whatever you're most comfortable with. If you're a fan of spreadsheets, you can use the downloadable budgeting spreadsheet I personally use by accessing the C&C Resource Pack at culturaandcash.com.

There are four pieces to figuring out the math for your budget:

1. How much do you own?

Start by taking inventory of how much money you have to your name. As of today, how much money do you have in your checking and savings accounts? What about cash? If the answer is zero, there is no shame in that. We all have to start somewhere. You are steps ahead of others by starting the process now.

Example:
Checking: $2,000, Savings: $500, Cash: $300

2. How much do you owe?

Next, understand what outstanding debt you have and the corresponding minimum payment. Factor in all debt, including student loans, medical debt, car loans, mortgages, credit card debt, etc.

Example:
Student loan: $40,000, min. payment $400
Car loan: $20,000, min. payment $300
Credit card debt: $5,000, min. payment $50

3. How much is coming in?

Now, compile any incoming money you receive on a *monthly basis.* This can include your salary from your job, alimony, side hustle income, etc.

Example:
Employment income: $4,000 ($2,000 biweekly)
Side hustle: $200

4. How much is going out?

This last step will take the longest, but it's probably the most important. Compile a list of your monthly expenses. Make sure to include all your bills and debt payments. This can seem like a daunting task if you have a lot of outgoing money. You can handle it. To make it easier, try separating your expenses into two categories: fixed and variable expenses.

Start by listing out your fixed expenses first. **Fixed expenses** stay the same month to month. For example, your rent payment should be the same in January as it is in February. It doesn't vary month over month.

Some examples of fixed expenses are housing, utility bills (internet, cell phone), transportation (car payments, car insurance), and healthcare premiums.

Example:
Housing: $1,500
Electricity: $50
Internet: $80
Cell phone bill: $50
Netflix: $20
Therapy copay: $60
Gym membership: $40
Prescriptions: $30
Car insurance: $70
Student loan: $40,000, min. payment $400
Car loan: $20,000, min. payment $300
Credit Card debt: $5,000, min. payment $50

Next, look at your **variable expenses**. As you may have guessed, variable expenses vary from month to month. For example, gasoline costs vary by how much you drive for the month or how much gas prices fluctuate.

Some examples of variable expenses are dining out, entertainment, self-care, clothing, travel, gifts, gasoline, groceries, pet supplies, and electricity. To estimate how much you're spending in these categories, download the last three months of statements from your credit card and debit card companies. Use these statements to review your past transactions and to take inventory of your spending history in those categories.

Example:
Groceries: $250
Dining out: $200
Entertainment: $100
Gasoline: $150
Electricity: $60
Self-care: $100
Beauty products: $50

Track Your Spending

You're doing great! You're off to a solid start with your budget. Now that you've gotten some clarity on how much money you own, owe, and comes in and comes out, you'll have to track your spending to make sure the budget you created reflects your **actual** spending.

My recommendation is to track your spending for a minimum of two months, but ideally, you'd do it for three. The reason for this is you will probably find you underestimated some of your spending. Let's say your initial budget review shows you spend $200 on entertainment, but the true number is closer to $300. You want your budget to reflect the real numbers, not the optimistic ones. Capturing the most accurate picture of your spending will allow you to set realistic budgeting goals. It will also save you the frustration that comes from having an imprecise budget.

To track your budget, download an app on your phone and

get in the habit of inputting and categorizing your spending as soon as you make a purchase. Just like you could use an app like MyFitnessPal to track what you eat, a budgeting app helps you track what you spend.

There are lots of apps on the market, but the ones I've had personal experience with and really liked are GoodBudget (free) and Envy (one-time $4.99 payment). They're user-friendly and allow you to categorize your transactions to capture your spending patterns accurately. Some people are big fans of apps or websites that sync to your debit and credit card and automatically categorize your transactions for you. Mint is a popular website that does this. I personally am not a fan. From my experience, their software tends to mislabel some transactions in the wrong category, which just creates extra work for you.

For example, let's say you have a transaction for concert tickets, but the software mistakenly logs it as food. You'd still have to go into the website and manually categorize it correctly. Who wants to do double work? Not me!

My two cents: If you're going to get stuck manually fixing errors, you might as well track them accurately yourself from the beginning on a budgeting tracker app. I'm always on the lookout and testing new budgeting apps to recommend to my social media community. If you'd like an updated list of my favorite budgeting apps to help you create a budget you can stick to, access the C&C Resource Pack.

Analyze and Adjust Your Spending

Once you've tracked your spending for two to three months, take the following steps:

1. **Evaluate:** Review the initial budget you created a couple of months ago and compare it to your actual spending. Are you satisfied with what you're spending on each spending category? Maybe by looking at your food spending, you've realized you're spending more money than you want on dining out. Maybe you overestimated how much you spend on gasoline. Adjust your budget numbers to make them closer to your desired spending. Remember, while it is important to cut back, it's also equally important to not over-restrict yourself of the things you love. Now that you have the real numbers, how much space do you have to make progress toward your financial goals, like paying off debt or increasing savings? $100 a month? $500 a month? More? Jot down your findings in your budget tracker.

2. **What if there's no money left over?** If there is little to no space left over at the end of the month, this means you have to cut back on your spending and increase your income to create the additional space. Don't feel bad; we all have to start somewhere. When I first did this exercise, I was lucky to have an extra $100 left over at the end of the month. In the next chapter, we'll talk about different ways you can create more space in your budget without burning out or making you feel too restricted.

3. **Revisit goals:** Now go back to the short-term goals that you wrote out earlier in this section. Let's say your goals include building a peace of mind fund, paying off your student loans, and saving for a vacation. If you have $600 left over at the end of the month to use toward your goals, decide how you want to allocate that money.

You could try some of these combinations to use the $600:

- $200 for the emergency fund, $200 extra payment for student loans, and $200 for the vacation fund.

- $400 for the emergency fund, $100 extra payment on student loans, and $100 for vacation.

- $300 for the emergency fund, $50 extra payment on student loans, and $250 for the vacation fund.

- Or any other combination that makes smart use of the extra $600 available to you.

USE SINKING FUNDS TO KEEP YOUR SPENDING ON TRACK

When thinking of your short-term goals, you also want to factor in sinking funds. Don't confuse sinking funds and peace of mind funds. Remember, a peace of mind covers **unforeseen** emergencies, like sudden job loss. A sinking fund is a smart way to save for a **projected expense.** They're good to use for big, irregular expenses.

Sinking funds work because you're putting money aside every month for a projected expense. By planning ahead for this future expense, you won't throw off your monthly spending.

One example of this is Christmas gifts. Christmas gifting only happens once a year, at the same time every year. Instead of scrambling to find the extra cash to buy gifts for loved ones or charging them on a credit card and getting yourself into debt, you can create a sinking fund.

Let's say you plan to spend $500 on Christmas gifts. If you divide the $500 by twelve months, you get around $42, which means if you save $42 every month for twelve months starting in January, by December, you will have the $500 needed to pay for gifts, worry and debt free! Now that's a reason to have some holiday cheer.

You can also use sinking funds to pay for other irregular expenses, like your yearly car insurance premium, vet expenses, vacations, and car maintenance. Identify what future spending you can create a sinking fund for and factor in sinking fund savings as a line item to your monthly spending.

4. **Choose a budgeting method:** Now that you've gotten clarity on your real spending patterns and decided how much extra cash you'll be using toward your short-term goals and any sinking funds, you'll need to pick a budgeting method to meet those goals. Here are some budgeting methods to try, listed from beginner to most complicated.

Four Budgeting Methods That Work

Envelope method: With the envelope method, also called the cash stuffing method, you'll divide up physical cash into separate envelopes that represent your spending categories. This is how it works. Let's say you budgeted $300 for entertainment a month. At the start of the month, you'll withdraw $300 from an ATM and place that cash in an envelope labeled "Entertainment." As you spend money on entertainment that month, use only cash from that specific envelope. Do not use your debit or credit card for entertainment expenses.

Once the $300 in cash is spent, *that's it*! No more spending on entertainment because you've reached your budgeted amount for the month. You have to have the discipline to respect that you've reached your spending goal and shouldn't pull money from a different envelope or charge it on a credit card.

This method is great if you tend to overspend. Switching to physical cash for your spending makes you more aware of your buying decisions. When you spend money by swiping a card or using mobile payment apps like Apple Pay or Google Pay it just doesn't feel as real. It's all digital and you never see real cash exchanged. Cash is as real as it gets, which makes you rein in impulse purchases.

If you don't want to have physical cash on you because you fear losing it, you can use an app like GoodBudget to use a virtual envelope method instead.

Online budget tool: Another great budgeting app to try is Much. It's founded by an Afro-Latina named Carmen Perez, and offers unlimited goal tracking, debt pay off tracking, and a digital community to keep you motivated—all in one. It costs $7.99 a month. I've also heard great things about Empower (formerly known as Personal Capital). Both these apps will offer free trials before you commit to a monthly subscription. Check them out!

Pay yourself first method: With this method, you set up all your bills and savings goals to be pulled out as soon as you get paid, and everything that's left over you spend worry-free.

For example, let's say you get paid twice a month, on the first and fifteenth of every month. You'd set up all your recurring bills (ex: rent, cell phone, internet, etc.) and savings targets (ex: $100 for vacation and $200 for the emergency fund) to be paid either on the first or the fifteenth. This way, all your bills and savings objectives are taken care of for the month as soon as your money comes in. The thought is that you can't spend what you don't have. So create a barrier for yourself by automating these money movements and setting everything on autopilot. This takes a little time to set up at first but once you've automated all your payments it will be the most hands-off budgeting method out of the four mentioned.

Spreadsheet: Now I know people go into fight mode when I mention spreadsheets, but this *is* a personal finance book so they deserve an honorary mention. If you like using spreadsheets, Microsoft Excel is a great tool to organize your finances. This is what I personally use. The spreadsheets do the math for you, and you can easily add different tabs every month to track your spending. Remember to visit culturaandcash.com to download the exact template I use for my monthly budgeting for free!

Finding the right budgeting method can be like shopping for new jeans. You'll have to try on different ones until you find the one that fits. Be patient with yourself and expect to make mistakes along the way. Stay committed to finding the best method that works for you, and use this powerful tool to make your dreams become a reality.

Budgeting with the Familia in Mind

Now as you work hard to get into the habit of budgeting and tracking your spending, keep in mind that any money you give to family should also be included in your budget as part of your spending plan. If you're regularly helping family with expenses but aren't tracking it as part of your budget, then you aren't capturing an accurate picture of your monthly spending. If it's important for you to factor your family into your budget, here are some strategies to try:

START THE CONVERSATION

Talk to your family. Let them know you are building better money management skills and want to include them in your spending. Ask them what kind of financial support they need and how often. Get details, do they need help paying a specific bill every month, or do they only need money when a financial emergency comes up? What kind of financial emergencies have they had in the past? How much did these emergencies cost? The answers to all these questions will help you better prepare to factor in financial support.

CREATE A LINE ITEM FOR A MONTHLY ALLOWANCE

Does your family require money on an ongoing basis? Factor them into your monthly budget the same way that you would any bill. Determine how much money you're able to help with, and commit to sending that same amount on time every month. Let's say you decided to provide a monthly allowance of $200 that you send them every fifteenth of the month. Add those $200 to your monthly spending for the month (under your fixed expenses). Be consistent and send them the money every fifteenth. The consistency will make it easier to follow your budget. You can easily transfer money to family with Zelle, Venmo, or in cash.

CREATE A SINKING FUND FOR THEM

In the previous chapter, we discussed peace of mind funds and how you can create one designated for extended family. If your family needs help covering big expenses, like paying for medical expenses or having the roof replaced, create a sinking fund and title it something like "Family Support Fund." Do you want to have $500 available for a family emergency? $1,000? Think of the specific number that works for your finances, divide it by twelve, and get in the habit of saving toward it every month.

OR SET THE BOUNDARY

Remember, a boundary is a healthy limit someone sets for themselves to protect their well-being. If you practiced the Quiero y Puedo approach and found you don't have the financial means to help or are choosing to focus on your financial goals, that's okay too. If your family pressures you into providing money you do not have or aren't willing to spend, practice kindness and tell them you'd love to help but are working on improving your finances first. Offer to help with your time or guidance instead. If you're ridiculed for acting intentionally with your money, remember you are not a *coda* or a broke bitch. Being a cycle breaker in your family is not easy, but you *can* do it. Maybe when the time is better, or money is more available, you can offer monetary support. "Not right now" doesn't mean no forever.

Your Financial Wellness Starts with Budgeting

In this chapter, we discussed how budgeting is a road map to help present you get to the future you want. A budget shouldn't restrict you. Instead, it should allow you to spend intentionally on what's important to you and cut back on what's not. It's a spending plan for your money.

Compared to the other pillars in the First Gen Five, budgeting will be the most challenging to adopt. That's the honest truth. The reason for this is that **mindful spending is an everyday practice.** You don't just get to set it and forget it. It's something you have to be committed to and be consistent with. This is why the majority of the chapter was dedicated to adopting the right money mindset and unlearning limiting beliefs that keep you from unleashing the power of budgeting.

Trust the process. Close yourself off from external pressures that want you to spend money on things that don't truly matter to you. When you have a vision and create a budget that's aligned with that vision, you'll have an easier time sticking to it.

It can take months or even years to get into the flow and ease of intentional spending. Be aware that with budgeting there is an element of trial and error. Be patient. You're going to make mistakes along the way, and that's expected. But when it happens, don't be too hard on yourself. It's part of the process. You can always do better the following month as long as you recommit to your why and have it visible to keep your dream alive. Because when you give your money a purpose, you're more mindful of where it's going.

Lastly, keep in mind you won't have to budget this intensely forever. Once you achieve important financial milestones, like paying off all your debt or building enough money to cover your peace of mind fund, you'll have extra money available to use on other financial goals or to elevate your quality of life. You'll have more breathing room to enjoy life's pleasures while knowing you've also built a solid financial foundation for yourself. But first, you got to put in the work to build that financial stability. Right now is that time, and future you will thank you for it!

Budgeting can be a lot easier when you have more disposable income available to you. But as First Gen with a different starting line, you likely have some debt that's limiting your ability to have disposable income. In the next chapter, we'll talk about the impact debt can have on your finances and how reducing your debt can improve your overall financial well-being. My goal in this upcoming chapter is to encourage you to take charge of your debt-payoff journey and teach you how to repay your debt more quickly. Because when you eliminate debt, you have more money to use on what really matters.

CHAPTER 5

DEBT SHOULD
FEEL UNCOMFY

My finances improve beyond my dreams.

I t was the fall of 2016, and I was looking for a room to rent in Carlsbad, a breezy coastal area in the northern region of San Diego, CA. I had started a new job a few months earlier and was looking to live nearby to have a shorter commute. I'd found a Craigslist post that matched what I was looking for posted by a woman by the name of Claire.

Claire's Craigslist post described her as a homebody, dog lover, and fitness enthusiast. *Sounds great so far*, I thought. When I met her to view the available room, I brought my dog, Bailey, to make sure she got along with her two slightly overfed black Labradors. The dogs sniffed butts and chased each other playfully in the backyard. Claire was friendly and patiently answered all my questions about the family-friendly neighborhood and the three-bedroom home she lived in. I'd be sharing the home with her.

Later that evening, I told my mom I had found a new place that checked all the boxes: It was a ten-minute drive from my new job, had a large yard for my dog, and the monthly rent cost was affordable. She looked at the pictures of Claire on Craigslist and turned to me in horror. She warned, "Don't move in with her, tiene cara de loca." I shrugged off her baseless opinion and signed the lease later that week.

My Nightmare Housemate

At first, our living situation was great. Claire worked part-time at a grocery store which meant she spent a lot of time at home. It felt comforting knowing Bailey had company while I was away at my desk job most of the day. When I arrived home, I was welcomed by the scent of cinnamon sticks and orange peels from the simmer pots Claire would boil on the stovetop. When I worked late, she'd leave me a note on the kitchen table that read, "Help yourself to some leftover soup."

Even though she was thirty years my senior, we had a nice roommate dynamic. We'd frequently spend evenings talking about our family back home or our challenges at work. I felt safe and at ease, and Bailey had new dog friends to play with. A month later, our new roommate, Jen, joined us. Jen was a childfree yoga instructor a few years older than me. She was laid-back, tidy, and respectful. The home felt like a Zen sanctuary and a nice respite from my demanding work hours.

But only a month and a half later, Jen informed me she was moving out. I was surprised to hear the news—I figured she must have gotten a new job in a different area, or maybe she'd gotten her own apartment for more privacy. "*Moving in with the boyfriend?*" I playfully teased with a grin on my face, wanting to get the tea on the new relationship. She shook her head and flashed an uncomfortable smile. She admitted that she didn't feel safe around Claire. My stomach sank, and I looked at her in confusion.

"*Claire spends all day drinking in her room,*" she whispered.

On two separate occasions, she'd seen her slam cabinets in the kitchen while mindlessly mumbling to herself and screaming at Jen unprovoked.

Jen was your typical yoga instructor—cool, calm, and collected—so I really couldn't make sense of why Claire would ever scream at her. This seemed so out of character, vastly different from the Claire I'd gotten to know in the last few weeks. But Jen spent a lot more time with Claire at home than I did since they both had flexible work schedules, and I was at the office all day.

Jen moving out so quickly raised a red flag inside me. First, my mom had said that she had una cara de loca. Now Zen Jen was saying Claire was frequently drunk and erratic. What was I missing?

It didn't take long until I got a taste of the real Claire. A few weeks later, she pulled me aside to angrily scold me and say I had to do a better job of cleaning the home. This was the first time she'd brought this up, so I was confused by her condescending and accusatory tone. I figured maybe she'd had a tough day at work, so I said I understood and I'd be happy to chat about cleaning expectations to make sure we were on the same page.

Later that evening, she handed me a list of daily, weekly, biweekly, and monthly cleaning duties. Immediately no! I can admit I'm no Marie Kondo, but I always make sure to tidy up after myself as I go. This list felt like I was a child given a chores list to earn a weekly allowance. Only there was no allowance at the end of the week. The way she snapped at me and the ridiculous list was a little jarring but not bad enough that I felt I couldn't live there anymore.

By the next week, Jen was out. Claire started acting more distant than usual. She dodged my eyes when I entered common spaces and spent a lot of time locked in her room alone. If I needed to ask her something, she coldly replied in one-word answers. The simmer pot days were long gone.

One evening, I was cleaning up after dinner when I opened the trash can and found it topped to the rim with a pile of empty Sutter Home mini wine bottles. There had to be twenty of them stuffed in the trash can. My mind filled with panic. Jen was telling the truth; Claire was an alcoholic!

Now I am no persinada. I drink and enjoy a good Michelada or Bellini with friends. But stacks and stacks of wine bottles seemed excessive and disturbing, especially from someone who claimed to live a healthy and fit lifestyle at our first meeting and on her Craigslist post. Claire was not who she portrayed herself to be, and it made me feel unsafe. What else could she be lying about?

That same night I started looking up new apartments, but all the options I found were expensive and outside of my budget. I was starting to get a little worried about my living situation. My home no longer felt like a safe haven. When driving home from work, I often wondered what version of Claire I would see at home. The sweet Claire who shares the dinner table with me and asks me about my day, or the rude, disheveled one who treats me like I called her mama a bitch?

I was living with a wild card. The unpredictability felt unsettling, especially when I knew that in a couple of months, I'd have to start studying for a rigorous work certification. I needed a safe and quiet space to live and study in so I could pass my exam. My home was like a minefield, and I constantly felt on edge as I anticipated Claire's next outburst. I opened up to a colleague at work about what was happening at home. She listened with horror in her eyes and urged me to leave ASAP. She even gifted me a pink pocket-sized pepper spray to protect myself with.

The last straw was when I came home early one day and found the house looking like it had been through an earthquake. The living room was turned upside down. There were blankets and pillows manically thrown all over the floor. The rugs were crinkled up, and all the house lights were off. Her dogs' water bowls had not a single drop of water in them. Her dogs were like her children, so this was especially alarming. I topped up the dogs' food and water bowls and looked for Claire, but she was nowhere to be found. The kitchen table was completely covered with half-opened mail showing "PAST DUE" and "TERMINATION NOTICE" in urgent bold-red font. Another one said something about foreclosure.

OMG. Claire was going through severe financial problems, which explained the excessive drinking and mood swings. Drinking issues, erratic behavior, and financial problems seemed like a recipe for disaster, and I wanted no part of it. These malas vibras were not it. I had to get away—and fast.

Desperately Seeking Affordable Options

The problem was that all the apartments I found in the area were almost twice what I was currently paying. I was paying $900 to rent a room, and I could hardly manage that. A one-bedroom apartment in the area would cost me at least $1,500. Rooming with another Craigslist random wasn't an option because I knew I needed stability for my upcoming exam and my mental well-being. I couldn't risk living with another wild card and having another bad roommate situation.

To make matters worse, almost none of the apartments I found accepted my sixty-pound Labrador mix, Bailey. I needed a new home ASAP, but affordable housing was almost impossible to find for my dog and me. My mind was racing with desperation. I needed a solution.

To make my problem worse, I only had around $1,000 in savings, not enough to cover a moving deposit and moving costs in San Diego County. My debt was out of control. I had a ton of student loans, credit card debt, and a car note, all of which were eating up most of my income. I had a prestigious white-collar job but was living paycheck to paycheck.

Although I had my parents' emotional support through this nightmare roommate situation, they didn't have the extra money to bail me out and help me find a safe new home. They couldn't help me pay for a portion of my new rent while I got back on my feet. They were hardly managing their own expenses. I felt completely helpless, stressed out, and on my own. I had a hard time sleeping at night, and my anxiety made it difficult for me to get through my workday. Is *this* what I had worked so hard for? To be stuck in situations where I felt like a helpless victim?

A Way Out

After weeks of desperately searching for a new home, I finally found a one-bedroom apartment that accepted a large breed of dog and that I could somewhat afford. I wouldn't have a lot of money left over at the end of the month, but I could manage to scrape by. I drove to tour the unit with high hopes.

The unit had popcorn ceilings, an old white electric stove, and cheap vinyl flooring. It was outdated, cramped, and musty. It wasn't an apartment I'd be proud of, but it was safe, close to work, and, most importantly, would be all mine and free of Claire.

I went back to the leasing office and cheerfully informed the leasing manager that I wanted to apply for the unit on the spot. I was so relieved my apartment search was finally over, and I'd finally have a safe space for me to live in. I was in the middle of the application process when the leasing manager tapped on my shoulder and politely told me, "Miss, I'm so sorry, the unit you just viewed and are applying to was just taken by another applicant."

A tidal wave of emotion hit me all at once. I buried my face in my hands and started sobbing deeply. I couldn't believe I had just lost this apartment. I had no money, no control of my circumstances, and now no apartment prospects. I had nothing.

The leasing manager was visibly taken aback. My reaction was so over-the-top. She probably thought, "*Wow, all this over an old apartment with popcorn ceilings?*" I'm sure she thought I was being a drama queen. But I'd been so stressed about moving and money for weeks that I was so relieved to have finally found a solution, only to have it taken away from me at a moment's notice. Fortunately, she was compassionate enough to talk to her manager and make an exception and get me a similar unit for the same price. I was out of Claire's home by the end of the month.

The Burden of Debt

As I look back at this difficult time in my life, I can clearly see how my poor money management skills had caught me with my pants down. I had no emergency savings and a ton of debt that took up the majority of my income. At the time, I didn't understand how debt was holding me back. I figured that as long as I could manage the minimum payments, I'd be okay, and the debt would eventually pay itself off with time. I didn't understand how debt could affect my lifestyle, my mental health, or my financial wellness. I didn't feel the urgency to pay it off.

As First-Gen, a lot of us start life in the negative. It's hard to avoid debt as a new adult when you come from nothing. Debt is almost a necessary evil in our journey to get ahead in life. I wouldn't have been able to attend college had I not taken student loans. I wouldn't have been able to easily get to my part-time job and drive to my college classes had it not been for a car loan. I don't regret taking on debt, but I wish I'd had a plan to control it. Instead, it controlled me.

This is why paying off debt is one of the five pillars in my First Gen Five framework. My goal in this chapter is to educate you on why debt should be treated like an emergency, to explain the benefits of a debt-free lifestyle, and to give you actionable tips to learn how to pay it off proactively.

What is debt?

In the simplest explanation, debt is borrowed money that needs to be paid back. Money is typically loaned by a financial institution, like a bank, credit union, or credit card company. Now these institutions don't loan you money out of the kindness of their heart. The reason they loan you money is that they get to *make money* off what they loaned you. They call this "interest." Interest is the price you pay for borrowing money. When you borrow money, you're expected to pay back the amount you borrowed—plus interest.

A Glimpse of Debt-Free Living

When I was riddled with debt, it was hard for me to picture life debt free. I'd had debt since I was seventeen and didn't even know what life as a debt-free adult felt like. Because it felt like a distant destination, it was hard for me to get excited about it or to give it much priority.

It wasn't until I had my horrible Craigslist roommate that I understood firsthand how debt was holding me back and having a negative impact on my life. I don't want you to have to learn the hard way like I did. As someone who is now proudly debt free, let me share some of the benefits I wish I'd known sooner of living a debt-free lifestyle:

- **More space to work on things that excite you:** Once your debt is paid off, any money that was being taken up for paying back debt is now freed up for *you* to use as you wish! This means your hard-earned money isn't going straight to creditors anymore. The extra money is called *disposable income*. You get to decide what to do with it. You no longer feel like you're working just to pay back the money you owe others. And it feels incredibly liberating! This is extra cash you can use to fund your life goals and dreams. You'll now have disposable income for that down payment on your first home or to treat yourself to that nice tropical vacation you've always dreamed of! You'll have extra money to generously support those who matter to you while still having plenty for yourself.

- **Less stress about money:** Once you become debt free, you'll feel a huge burden lifted off your shoulders. You'll be more financially secure and will have more power to avoid toxic situations like a bad roommate or a bad boss. Debt no longer owns you. Your physical and mental health will improve because you'll have more wiggle room in your finances and won't feel as cash-strapped as you did when you had debt. With debt, you feel like you're swimming against the current. You can take broader strokes and kick as hard as you want, but at the end of the day, you still feel tired and like you didn't make much progress. When you're debt free, it feels like you're on a floaty chilling down a lazy river on a sunny day with a margarita in hand. Debt-free living is elite!

- **Increased flexibility and lifestyle choices:** Now my favorite benefit! With a debt-free lifestyle, you'll have more flexibility to say yes to *you*. You'll get to decide where to live, what kind of career moves you can make, and what kind of lifestyle to live. A big reason why I was able to quit my stable corporate job to become a full-time TikToker was because I was debt free. Since I had no debt, my living expenses were lower, which meant I didn't need much money to cover my basic necessities. That meant I was able to take risks with my career and switch to a new industry, even if I wasn't making much money at first. When I was up to my neck in debt, I needed an extra $900 just to cover my debt obligations. There is zero chance I would have left my steady job for the unknown if I still had thousands of dollars of debt. Debt would have held me back. And what a waste of my talent that would have been. Living a simpler lifestyle with little to no debt lets you design a life where you're in the driver's seat. Your debt doesn't call the shots—you do!

ACTIVITY: ENVISION YOUR DEBT-FREE LIFE

Now take some time to dream about how you'll use your extra cash once you become debt free. First, get a rough idea of how much of your monthly money is going to debt right now. When you eliminate your debt, the money will be completely freed up for you to use however you want.

What will you do with it? What financial goals will you use the extra cash for? Will you use some of the extra money to buy products or services that make your life easier?

Keep these answers in mind and use them as motivation as you read through the rest of this chapter.

Limiting Beliefs about Debt

You are worthy of a debt-free and abundant life. It's waiting for you! But before you embark on this journey, we need to clear out some of the mindset blocks from both society and our upbringing that can hold you back from seeing debt as the emergency that it is.

What messaging have you heard about debt at home? I'll go first.

"DEBT IS NORMAL."

This is a belief I inherited from my parents. I remember when I decided to get serious about paying off my debt. I excitedly shared my plans with my mom. Instead of hearing encouragement from her and getting praise for making better money choices, I heard, "What's the point? You're always going to have debt in some shape or form." My excitement was shot down and deflated.

As of this writing, I've been debt free for three years, so the notion that "You'll always have debt" is simply not true. I now know that firsthand.

But back when my mom told me this, I didn't have that lived experience. I was younger, impressionable, and not as experienced with money management. I thought maybe she's right. After all, she's my mom and has been on this earth longer than I have. She must know what she's talking about. Now that I've experienced the benefits of a debt-free lifestyle, I'm so relieved I had the determination to reject that limiting money belief and break that generational cycle. This is why it's important to surround yourself with a like-minded community who are supportive and can cheer you on while you're working on improving your finances.

I don't fault my mom for having that negative money mindset. I have compassion for her. The system was not created for her to thrive in it. She was never taught financial literacy, and our capitalist society preyed on her and other marginalized groups to spend and consume at the expense of her financial well-being. But just because someone is family or older than you, it doesn't mean you should take what they say as the law.

"I'M NEVER GOING TO PAY IT OFF."

I frequently hear this one from money-coaching clients and recently from a client with $200,000 in student debt. I completely empathize with someone who feels that way—$200,000 is a lot of money, and it can feel like pushing a big heavy boulder up a steep hill. In some parts of the country, you can buy a home with that amount of cash! It's even more demoralizing when you realize more privileged people like the Privileged Pattys and Average Amys got to dodge debt or minimize their debt while we are stuck dealing with the financial burden. I think it's almost criminal that someone can gamble their money away at a casino and file for bankruptcy, but a student who pursued a higher education for a chance at a better life is shackled with student loans for life. Until public policy changes, we are stuck with student loans, so the best we can do is learn how to manage them.

My advice for anybody who feels overwhelmed by their debt: Take a moment to pause, breathe, and affirm to yourself—you have everything you need to accomplish anything you want. You can pay off this debt, but it will take a plan, time, consistent work, and patience. I will teach you how.

Latines and Their Cars

In addition to our limiting money beliefs, I've also observed that Latines' obsessions with cars keep us in the cycle of debt. Since I can remember, I've always heard my family describe success by what someone drives. Just the other day, when I was visiting family, my nana was telling me about a neighbor's daughter and how successful she is. "Le va muy bien. Trabaja en el gobierno y trae un carro del año."

In America, I think it's common to describe someone's success by their title and employer. It sounds something like saying, "Oh, and she's a VP at Goldman Sachs," or "She's a director at Microsoft." I've never heard someone in America add, "And they drive a new Tesla." But for some reason, it's what our community considers a marker of success.

We need to have an honest conversation about the chokehold cars have in the Latine community. We place too much value on what kind of car we drive. As mentioned earlier, my theory is that since a lot of us didn't have access to financial literacy, we mistakenly believe we need to show our wealth by what's visible.

Does everyone have access to your bank statement to see how much money is in your checking account? No, but anyone can see what type of car you drive up in at the family carne asada. And that's what you're measured by. Remember, in Chapter 2, I mentioned my dad owns four cars? He has the four cars as a status symbol, showing anyone driving by his home that he's el mas chingón de toda la cuadra.

But a car shouldn't be viewed as an investment or a status symbol. A true investment increases in value over time. A car is a depreciating asset, which means it **loses** value over time. If you buy a car this year, in five years it will be worth less, not more. As a matter of fact, new cars lose value as soon as they're driven off the dealer's parking lot. Instead of *making* you money, a car *costs* you money in the form of car insurance, maintenance, repairs, registration fees, gasoline, and car payment.

A CAR IS NOTHING MORE THAN A TOOL

A car should be viewed as a tool you need to drive from point A to point B. Don't fall for the marketing schemes that say you need a new luxury car to live a happy life.

Two of my best friends fell for these advertising ploys and bought matching white BMWs. They constantly complain about the high maintenance costs and half-jokingly say they want to light their cars on fire to cash out on the car insurance settlement (BTW, don't do this, this is called insurance fraud). They're not worth the headache. The goal is to drive something that's safe, reliable, and reasonably inexpensive to maintain. A practical car like a Honda Civic or a Toyota Camry are tried-and-true vehicles that are cost-effective to buy and upkeep.

You shouldn't tie your level of success or self-worth to the kind of car you drive, even though you may have grown up hearing otherwise. What kind of car do you think the average million-aire drives? Mercedes, Ferrari, or BMW? According to a study by Experian Automotive, 61 percent of wealthy people drive a Ford, Toyota, or Honda.[1] Rich people, they're just like us! But in all seriousness, they understand it doesn't make financial sense to spend a lot of money on a car that's going to lose value over time. Instead of driving fancy cars, they drive modest cars and invest the difference in the stock market, a business, or real estate. That's how you build true wealth.

AVOID ONGOING CAR DEBT

Most traditional personal finance books will tell you to buy a lightly used, reliable, two-to-three-year-old vehicle. This is because they don't have the high maintenance costs of older vehicles since they're still relatively new and cost significantly less than a new car at the dealer.

With the pandemic, the low supply of cars has made used cars just as expensive as new ones. I've had two cars, and both were bought new. Not because I wanted something del año but because I knew

---

1   Pan, Jing. "'Not Living Their Life to Impress Others': These Are the Top Car Brands that Rich Americans Earning More than $200k Drive Most—Here's Why You Should Steer toward Them Too." Yahoo, April 16, 2023. https://www.yahoo.com/now/not-living-life-impress-others-140000227.html#:~:text=According%20to%20a%202022%20study,Other%20studies%20show%20similar%20results.

I lived far from family, and if I had any mechanical issues, I'd be on my own to handle them with an untrustworthy mechanic. If you buy new, the smart thing to do is to drive that thing until the wheels fall off.

In my family, it's a very common practice to buy a new car with a five-year loan, and once that loan is paid up, go back to the dealer and treat yourself to a newer model.

A conversation about this came up with my family a couple of years ago. I excitedly told them I was a few months away from paying off the car note for my 2011 Toyota Corolla. My uncle said, "Good for you! So what car are you buying next?" That's not the point! This is how you stay stuck in the cycle of debt!

Instead of taking on another car loan, be smart with the extra cash freed up to you from no longer having a car payment (a.k.a. your new disposable income). You can use the extra money to build savings, pay off other debt, or invest. That is how you improve your finances. Not by digging a hole and getting yourself into new car debt.

My family bullied me for years for driving my paid-off Corolla. They said I should treat myself to a new car and have something I was proud of driving and being seen in. I patiently explained that I was using the extra cash to pay off debt, but it didn't matter to them. All they saw was that I was being a coda and didn't want to spend money on a new car, even though my Corolla was in perfectly fine condition.

It didn't feel good to be teased by my family. But I no longer let others make financial decisions for me, and you shouldn't either. Don't let others pressure or ridicule you into making money moves that you can't truly afford—even if it is family.

Is all debt bad?

We've spent the majority of this chapter talking about how debt can hold you back from the fabulous and abundant life you're destined to live. We also covered some of the limiting beliefs that can keep you from handling debt more aggressively.

Now, let's go over different types of debt and how they impact you. Some types of debt are worse than others. Here are three types of debt you should know.

DEBT FOR NOTHING

The types of debt that fall into this category are credit card debt and consumer loans. This is the worst kind of debt you can have! Avoid it like the plague. If you have this kind of debt, prioritize paying it off over other types of debt. It's also known as "bad debt."

Debt for nothing usually comes about from excessive consumerism, like overspending on clothes, furniture, dining out, or buying the latest gadgets.

The reason I call it debt for nothing is that although spending money on these items does give you a quick hit of dopamine when buying, they aren't increasing your net worth or helping you build generational wealth in the long term.

Getting into credit card debt for an Instagrammable trendy fall wardrobe isn't going to make you money or increase your net worth. In ten years, you'll have nothing of true value to show for that debt. If it's not helping you build long-term wealth, you should avoid getting into debt for it. If you don't have the cash for it, then you can't really afford it.

This type of debt can typically be avoided by creating a spending plan and buying the items with cash—and avoiding any interest payments. What makes this type of debt worse is that it usually comes with higher interest rates (usually in the double digits) which means the items cost you more to buy. Debt for nothing is usually impulsive and is made in the name of instant gratification. You can also accumulate debt for nothing from emotional overspending, as an unhealthy way to cope with loss or grief.

If you have this kind of debt, I don't want you to feel shame for it. Have some compassion for yourself. You're already doing better by reading this book and taking ownership of your money journey. But understand that carrying this type of debt will make it incredibly hard to make real progress toward your financial goals. This is your break-glass-in-case-of-emergency moment. You need to prioritize paying off this debt first—more on how to pay off this type of debt later in this chapter.

DEBT THROUGH EMERGENCIES

The types of debt that fall into this category include medical debt, credit card debt after being laid off, or debt from an unforeseen accident. Life happens, and sometimes when life throws a curveball at us, our finances take a hit. That's okay. You can prepare yourself for life's ups and downs by having the proper insurance and having a peace of mind fund in place, as discussed in Chapter 3.

DEBT FOR YOUR FUTURE

The types of debt that fall into this category are student loans, mortgages, and business loans. While it's the least bad of the three to have, be cautious and thoughtful before taking it on.

This type of debt is usually necessary to make large purchases like attending college or buying a home—an investment in your future. Unless you have rich parents or hit the lotto, the majority of us are going to have to take on this type of debt to make these large purchases.

Attending college should give you a higher earning potential than someone who didn't attend college. It's an investment in your education that should pay off in the long term. Taking out a mortgage helps you buy a home to live in and gives you an asset (the home) you can eventually sell off for money. Taking out a business loan to open your own coffee shop can be an investment in the future if your business succeeds and is profitable.

Investment debt usually comes at a lower interest rate. For example, some of my federal student loans had an interest rate of 6 percent, which is much lower than the double-digit interest rates of debt for nothing. Debt for your future is usually well thought-out and part of a long-term vision to improve your financial future.

Other financial experts will call this debt "good debt." I hate that term. Calling this type of debt "good debt" caused me and other Millennials to be reckless with student loans. I took out more student loans than I needed for college because I didn't understand how loans and interest truly worked. But back in high school, one of my teachers claimed student loans were "good debt." This was the only reference I had to student debt, that it was "good debt."

When the financial aid offered me money in student loans, I figured, well, it's the good kind of debt, so yes, more of that, please! *Debt is still debt.* All debt holds you back from using your money toward your personal life goals and dreams and should be avoided or mitigated when possible.

How to Pay Off Debt

In this chapter, we've discussed how debt puts a drag on your finances, the benefits of a debt-free lifestyle, how to overcome limiting beliefs about our ability to pay off debt, how buying new cars keeps us in the cycle of debt, and the three types of debt you can have.

By now, you should feel eager to make a more concerted effort to slay your debt. But what if you don't have extra cash to pay off your debt more aggressively? Here are three things you can do to free up more money to pay off debt:

1. **Decrease your spending:** If you feel like you have no room to make extra payments beyond the minimum payments on your debt, try looking into ways to decrease your spending.

Can you reduce your housing expenses by temporarily moving in with a roommate or moving back home? Can you switch your cell phone plan from a traditional wireless provider to a prepaid provider? Can you cut back on your eating out and save money by cooking at home more often? Remember, hay comida en la casa. Can you cancel subscription services you aren't using to save some extra cash? According to CNBC, 42 percent of people have forgotten that they're still paying for a subscription they no longer use. Who really needs that many subscriptions? That's a lot of potential savings!

Get creative and think about all the different ways you can reduce your spending. Review and analyze what you're spending money on, and trim out the extra fat. Your budget review from the previous chapter will help with this.

If you review your spending patterns and find you only have an extra $50 to use toward debt, that's okay. The goal is to use any extra money to pay more than the required minimum payment. For example, if your minimum payment is $200 but you make a payment of $250, that extra payment of $50 will help you pay off your balance quicker and get out of debt faster.

2. **Increase your income:** If your spending is already lean, then consider increasing your income instead. Can you speak to your supervisor at work and make yourself available for overtime hours? Or maybe it's time to find a new role altogether and give yourself a pay raise. Job hopping is one of the easiest ways to gain a significant salary increase. According to the BBC, job switchers were able to receive a 12 percent raise by job hopping.[2] It sure beats the measly 2 to 3 percent annual raise your employer will probably give you for staying in your current role. Or can you pick up a side gig like babysitting your neighbor's kids to make extra cash? Could you sign up to deliver groceries on Instacart or pick up some shifts as a bartender at a local restaurant?

There is a limit on how much you can trim your spending, but there is no cap on how much you can grow your income. Start exploring new ways to earn extra money and use the extra cash to attack that debt. You can do this!

3. **Decrease your spending, and increase your income:** If you can swing doing both at the same time, it's like adding gasoline to a fire.

That's how I turbocharged my debt repayment. I made the sacrifice to move out of state from San Diego, CA, to Phoenix, AZ. I didn't want to leave the beautiful California coast. I had all my friends and family there. In Phoenix, I knew nobody, and to make it worse, the summer weather was scorching hot, and the state was full of gun-toting, red MAGA-hat wearers. But I knew I had to

---

2   Christian, Alex. "The Case for Job Hopping." Worklife, July 21, 2022. https://www.bbc.com/worklife/article/20220720-the-case-for-job-hopping.

temporarily change my lifestyle to improve my finances, and moving out of state was the fastest way for me to do it.

This is how moving to Arizona accelerated my debt repayment. The cost of living is 31 percent lower in Phoenix than it is in San Diego. With my housing costs being lower, I was able to decrease my spending and use the extra savings toward paying off my debt. I also increased my income with my new job in Phoenix. My new role came with a $10,000 pay raise, which meant I had additional money to use toward my debt. I decreased my spending by lowering my housing costs while increasing my income by finding a better-paying job. Double yay!

If you can't pull off option #3 right now, don't feel discouraged. Doing one of the three I mentioned above is still better than ignoring your debt and just making the minimum payments. Focus on what you can do, and strategize the best way you can put that extra money toward paying off your debt.

Pick a Debt-Payoff Strategy

Now that we've covered different ways you can create more space to pay down your debt let's discuss how you'll strategically use the extra money. If you're ready to slay your debt, here are four practical steps to follow:

1. **Organize your debt:** First, go to culturaandcash.com to access the C&C Resource Pack and download my free debt tracker. Use the fillable workbook to organize your debt by name, outstanding balance, minimum payment, interest charge, and payment date. The tracker will help you follow along with your own finances and will give you a clear picture of where all the bodies are buried.

Factor in all debt, including student loans, medical debt, car loans, mortgages, credit card debt, etc. We already did some of this work in Chapter 4, "Budgeting Is Your BFF." Don't let the math scare you. I promise it's simple! I kept the numbers nice and round, so they'll be easy to follow. Let's walk through them together with the example below.

Example: Sonia has the following three debts:
Student loan: $10,000, min. payment of $400, 5% interest
Car loan: $2,000, min. payment of $300, 10% interest
Credit card debt: $5,000, min. payment of $50, 20% interest

2. **Pick a debt-repayment strategy:** Out of the three debts above, which one should Sonia tackle first? Should she focus on one over the other? Or should she focus equal efforts on paying them all off? Someone with limited money skills might see the example above and be immediately drawn to paying off the biggest debt—the student loan debt at $10,000.

Student loan: $10,000, *min. payment of $400*, **5% interest**
Car loan: $2,000, min. payment of $300, 10% interest
Credit card debt: $5,000, min. payment of $50, 20% interest

At first, it might make sense to pay off the loan with the biggest balance. But when comparing that debt to the other two, you'll notice that the loan has the smallest interest charge at only 5 percent, which makes the cost of borrowing money relatively cheap.

Even though the balance is the highest, because the interest is lower, the debt is *cheaper* than the rest. This doesn't mean you should wait the full ten years to pay off student loans because, remember, debt is still debt, and all debt holds you back. But since it's the cheapest debt on your list, it shouldn't be your first priority to tackle.

Instead, it will be smarter to use either the debt snowball or debt avalanche method.

HOW THE DEBT SNOWBALL METHOD WORKS

With this method, you focus on paying off the debt with the *smallest balance* first.

Following our example above, this means Sonia should focus on the car loan of $2,000 since it has *the smallest balance* of the three.

Student loan: $10,000, min. payment of $400, 5% interest
Car loan: $2,000, *min. payment of $300, 10% interest*
Credit card debt: $5,000, min. payment of $50, 20% interest

Using this strategy, Sonia would pay minimum payments on the student loan and credit card debt, $400 and $50, respectively, and focus all extra payments on the car loan.

WHY IT WORKS

The snowball method works because you'll pay off the loan with the smallest balance relatively quickly. It's a lot faster to pay off a loan of $2,000 versus $10,000. A bigger balance takes longer to pay off.

Once you pay off that first loan, you're going to feel instant gratification for having one less debt to worry about. Your three debts now went to two! This win will give you the motivation you need to keep making progress toward paying off your debt. They call it the snowball method because the momentum to pay off your debt will snowball and lead to more positive change. You'll get a little pep in your step and feel more confident about your money management skills. If you've paid off one debt, you have what it takes to pay off the rest.

Any plant mom will understand this analogy. It's kind of like when you manage to keep your first house plant alive. When you maintain the first one, you wonder, Well, what other types of plants can I handle? You start doing some research and decide to graduate from low-maintenance succulents to needier plants because you know you can keep them alive now. Next thing you know, you're in a home full of plantitas. Knowing you have the skills to keep the first plant alive gives you the confidence to take on more in the future.

HOW THE DEBT AVALANCHE METHOD WORKS

With this method, you focus on paying off the debt with the *largest interest* first.

Following our example above, this means Sonia would focus on the credit card with an interest charge of 20 percent since it has *the largest interest* of the three.

> *Student loan: $10,000, min. payment of $400, 5% interest*
> *Car loan: $2,000, min. payment of $300, 10% interest*
> *Credit card debt: $5,000, min. payment of $50,* **20% interest**

Using this strategy, she'd make minimum payments on the student loan and car loan, $400 and $300, respectively, and focus all extra payments on the credit card balance.

WHY IT WORKS

The reason this strategy works is because it will *save* you the most money in interest charges. Since it's the debt with the highest-interest charge, it's the most expensive debt out of the three. This makes the most mathematical sense to avoid the most interest charges you can. Who wants to pay more money to these creditors? Not me! If you're motivated by saving money in the long run, this might be a better strategy for you.

With this method, your progress won't be as fast as the debt snowball strategy. With the snowball method, you target the *smallest* debt balance first, knowing it's going to be *faster* to pay off than a bigger balance. For example, a $500 balance can be paid off in a couple of months, whereas a $5,000 balance might take years to pay off.

That means that if you choose to use the debt avalanche method, you have to feel comfortable seeing a large balance until it's paid off. The benefit of the avalanche method is knowing you saved the most money in interest costs by targeting the highest-interest debt first—the most expensive debt on your list.

So which method is better? It depends! What motivates you more?

Is it seeing your debt decrease from three loans to two? Then the debt snowball might be a good fit!

Or are you more motivated by knowing you saved the most money? That's the case for me. Mentally, I'm okay knowing I won't see a "$0 balance" any time soon. I feel happier knowing I saved the most money in interest charges in the long run and raised my middle finger to the credit card companies.

Think about which of these methods resonates with you, pick a strategy, and get started. I'm rooting for you!

3. **Pay more than the minimum:** To recap, the first step to paying off debt is first getting all your debt organized, which includes understanding what types of debt you owe, the outstanding balance, minimum payments, and interest rates. My free debt organizer helps with that. The second step is to choose a debt-repayment strategy, either the debt snowball

or debt avalanche method. Once you've completed those steps, step #3 is to commit to paying more than the minimum payment.

It will be nearly impossible to get out of debt if you keep paying the minimum payment, especially if it's high-interest debt like credit card debt.

Paying the minimum payment might seem convenient. It's a smaller payment, which means more money for you now. But the smaller payment comes at a big price to future you! Paying the minimum payments keeps you in debt longer, which means you'll end up paying more money in interest charges. This will cost you much more in the long run and will make it harder for you to make positive progress toward more fulfilling financial goals.

Let's say your minimum payment is $50. Instead of just paying the $50, throw any extra cash you have toward paying off the balance. Even if it's an extra $20, it will still help you pay off the debt more quickly than if you just paid the minimum payment.

4. **Patience is key. Reward yourself along the way:** Lastly, be patient! You didn't accumulate this debt overnight. So it's unrealistic to think it will be paid overnight.

The best way to pay off debt is slow and steady. Set up micro-goals and stay consistent. Be kind to yourself, stay focused, and keep making those extra payments! When you start feeling like you're losing motivation, remind yourself why becoming debt free is important to you and use it as momentum. Reward yourself as you make progress by treating yourself to a relaxing pedicure or a celebratory drink with a friend. Find a like-minded community that's also focused on its debt-payoff journey to keep yourself accountable. The C&C Resource Pack includes access to an exclusive Discord channel where you can meet and get support from other readers of this book. Celebrate your payoff wins on social media. Most people will be happy for you and cheer you along. You can do this.

Navigating Debt with Your Familia

Now that we've learned what debt is, the benefits of living a debt-free life, and strategies to pay it off for good, let's talk about how to navigate debt with your family.

As First-Gen, it's not uncommon for our family to tap us on the shoulder and ask us to take out a loan on their behalf. As we covered in Chapter 2, we operate as a collectivist culture. We are communal people, so going to our family when we need support is a natural choice. Financial institutions aren't exactly warm and welcoming to immigrants with limited financial means. It's hard to find a bilingual speaker they can trust, and all the legal paperwork can be intimidating to sift through. Their income or credit score may be low, and they know you'll have an easier time getting approved for a loan anyway. It's much easier to call on their daughter or niece la que gana bien.

Navigating debt with family can get tricky! One of my friends, let's call her Marissa, told me she had a big fight with her family because she wasn't willing to take out a car loan for her younger cousin. Marissa is the most financially stable in her family and has a good credit score, so naturally, the family turned to her. She told her family she wasn't comfortable with the arrangement, and they angrily told her she was a mal agradecida and a bad cousin/niece. It caused friction in her family and made her feel taken advantage of.

Before taking out a loan for family, whether it's for business, a car, or a mortgage, think of the following:

1. **Understand the consequences:** Taking out a loan is a big financial commitment. In a perfect world, you'd take out the

loan, your family member would make timely payments, and the loan would be paid off quickly. But we don't operate in a perfect world, so it's important to understand what could happen in the worst-case scenario.

Let's say Marissa had taken out a car loan for her cousin. But six months later, her cousin was fired from her job at Subway and could no longer make the car payments. The loan still needs to be paid. And since Marissa took out the loan in her name, she'd be on the hook for making the payments. If Marissa doesn't make the payments, her credit score will suffer. After enough missed payments, the bank will forcibly take the car back in what's called a repossession. A repossession will have a serious impact on your credit score. It can affect your credit for up to seven years!

Maybe Marissa can manage to make the payments but at the expense of her own financial wellness. Because she's having to make extra payments on her cousin's car, she has less money to save for her down payment fund. Now she doesn't have money to catch up with friends over dinner. Now she's living paycheck to paycheck, or even worse—she's getting herself into debt to meet all her financial obligations. All this trouble for a car that wasn't even hers.

Taking on debt for someone else will also make you less desirable to lenders. Your credit score may take a dip since it shows you're under more debt, and lenders will think it's riskier to loan you money. Let's say that in a year, you want to buy a new car for yourself. Because your credit history shows you have your cousin's car debt as your own, you may have to pay higher interest on your car loan—or even worse—straight up get denied for a loan.

If you cosign on a mortgage for a family member, when it's time for *you* to buy *your* first home, you may miss out on first-time home-buyer benefits. These include extra tax deductions or first-time home-buyer programs. The home you bought as a favor to your family would be viewed as your "first home," even though it's technically not.

Lastly, in this worst-case scenario, if the loan goes south, it can ruin your relationship with that loved one. I think anyone who decides to loan money to family does it with the best intentions. But if someone stops making payments and becomes a *mala paga,* would you be angry at them or resent them? Would you feel comfortable knowing this could forever change your relationship?

This is my personal rule: I don't loan money I can't afford to lose. If I decide to loan money to a loved one, I see it as a gift. I choose to loan money because it brings me joy to be able to help someone I care about (if I can financially afford to, of course). But I understand humans are complicated beings and don't feel the same urgency to pay back someone they know as they do a big bank. Naturally, there is more flexibility with a human being than with a global financial institution.

If I loan money, I'm not expecting it back. If I do get it back, it will be a pleasant surprise. Back in my Craigslist roommate days, I couldn't afford to gift money. If this is the case for you, then it's time to set the boundary. More about that in a bit.

2. **Come up with a repayment plan:** If you practice the Quiero y Puedo approach and decide that taking out a loan for a family member is the right choice for you, I'd suggest you have an open and honest conversation about your expectations. Explain why you agreed to help and that you're hoping for the best, but have a transparent discussion about the consequences of falling behind on payments.

   Come up with a payment schedule. Do you prefer they make payments to the bank directly? Do they need to email you proof of payment for your records? Or do you feel more comfortable with them sending you the money in advance and you make the payment yourself?

Get clear on when the payment due dates are, the payment amount, and the timeline for when it should be paid off. Word of caution: Proposing a written agreement might not go over well. Your family will view it as too formal and may feel offended because they think a contract is a sign that you don't trust them. If you feel uneasy loaning the money without an agreement, listen to your gut and offer help in other ways.

3. **Set the boundary:** I've had to set this boundary with both my parents. My dad recently asked me to take out a mortgage on his behalf. He said, "Don't worry, mija, I'll make the payments, and when the house is paid off, I'll leave it to you as thank you." (Okay, generational wealth!) I trust my dad and know he's committed to paying back the money he owes. He'd take up an extra job and suffer in silence before missing a payment, so I wasn't concerned about him being a mala paga. I love my dad, but I told him I couldn't do him that favor because I knew it would put a strain on my finances and affect my eligibility for first-time home-buyer benefits for my first home. I could tell he was a little disappointed, but he understood and didn't pressure me to change my mind. This is the best-case scenario. Your family makes the ask, you politely decline, and they understand and move on.

Your family may not be as understanding. I've had those experiences too, and they're tough to live through. Sometimes you turn into the black sheep for prioritizing your finances, and you need to be okay with that. It's not easy.

But understand it doesn't make you a bad daughter or a bad

family member. You can offer support in other ways. If they're open to receiving another type of support, tell them you're happy to spend time with them crafting a budget or offering resources so they can learn how to improve their credit score and can secure loans on their own.

Ultimately the choice is yours whether to take on debt for your family. I would personally only agree to take on debt for someone else if I knew I could manage the payments on my own and knew I wouldn't resent them later. Whatever your choice is, let it be a decision you made on your own because it aligns with your values, priorities, and financial ability, and not because someone else is guilting you or pressuring you into doing it. This can take time to master, but the more you practice honest money conversations with family, the easier it gets.

You Can Crush This Debt!

In this chapter, we covered how debt, although a necessary evil for most First-Gen, can put a strain on our finances and make it harder to reach our financial goals. It's harder to save for a new home, replace our car, or pay for a graduate degree if the majority of our income is being eaten away by debt. A debt-free lifestyle gives you more flexibility and allows you to design a life with intention.

We discussed some of the most common limiting beliefs about paying off debt and how we can overcome them. We covered the different types of debt you can have, ways to come up with extra cash to pay it off sooner, and different methods to pay off your debt balance strategically. We also explored how you can navigate loaning money to family, whether it's by coming up with a plan for them to repay you or by implementing financial boundaries.

Debt can feel like the least "sexy" of the First Gen Five pillars.

But paying off debt is as equally important as planning and saving for the future. And remember, every time you pay off a debt balance, you have more cash to use on things that matter. Once you've put in the work and made it to the other side of your payoff journey, you'll feel a new sense of confidence and accomplishment. The future version of you deserves this!

In the next chapter, we'll do a deep dive into how building a strong credit score can give you options when you most need them. Building a healthy credit score can be accomplished a lot faster than paying off large sums of debt, saving for a peace of mind fund, or investing for the future. It's an easy win and one that can come with a lot of savings and perks. Let's get to work!

CHAPTER 6

CREDIT BUILDING: OUTSMART THE CREDIT CARD COMPANIES

I am capable of achieving wealth and success.

The glamour of Hollywood and spotting A-list celebrities in the wild. The Santa Monica pier and warm beach days. Hiking and sweating it up at Runyon Canyon. These were all things I was looking forward to as a new transplant living in LA. I had just graduated from college earlier that summer and moved to the greater Los Angeles area for my first big-girl job. While my classmates bitched and moaned about the college days being over and having to work in "the real world," I felt very accomplished and eager to start adulting in a diverse and fast-paced metropolis.

I was the first in my family to graduate from college and had managed to land a professional job with no connections in corporate America. I was living in a vibrant new city and had plenty of friends in town with whom I could explore my new stomping grounds. While some of my friends had the option to move back home, I had to get my first apartment all to myself, a small former basement converted into a studio apartment in Pasadena, CA. I felt independent, prepared, and hopeful for my new chapter.

A Concerned Older Sister

It was then that I started feeling guilty about my younger brother Carlos. His situation was far from mine. He'd dropped out of high school a few years earlier and didn't have any solid plans for his future. He was 21, living at home in our small border town, and had no prospects to look forward to. I wanted to help my brother achieve success like I did. I wondered if a change of scenery could help him get unstuck. Maybe if he moved in with me, to a big city like Los Angeles, he'd be inspired by all the opportunities and find his path. I suggested he move in with me, and within a month, he left Mexicali and made the four-hour drive up to relocate to LA.

Another Difficult Housemate

Well, as the saying goes, no good deed goes unpunished. My brother was not the roommate I expected him to be. Like most Latines, he was used to my mom cooking and cleaning up after him (even as a grown-ass man), so he never learned how to "adult." I had foolishly assumed that as a guest in my home, he'd be on his best behavior and pick up better habits to demonstrate his gratitude. I knew he was a slob—I'd lived with him for almost twenty years. But his messiness didn't bother me as much when we lived under my mom's roof. My mom's home was a larger house, so his mess was always out of sight and out of mind. I had my own clean space away from his cochinero.

This was a big difference from the small studio apartment we shared. We had no walls. Zero privacy. Now remember from my previous chapter, I am no clean freak. I'll be the first to admit that. But he was *filthy*. He left his dirty clothes sprawled all over the floor and left his food-encrusted morning dishes in the sink for hours, stinking up the small space. I worked all day at my office job, and after being done with my commute and errands, I wanted to sit back and relax and enjoy my evening, not come home to a dirty apartment with *his* mess. I was prepared to share space but this—¡no mames! *This* is not what I signed up for.

We argued constantly about cleaning expectations. I wasn't asking him to be my butler or welcome me home with a five-course meal. The original agreement was that he could come to live in LA with me—rent-free—if he found a part-time job and cleaned up after himself. The expectation was that once he got a job and could sustain himself, he'd move out to his own place.

After endless arguments and no resolution, I told my brother that I made a mistake in inviting him to live with me. One, I didn't have the space. Since the studio apartment didn't have any walls, I slept on the bed, and he slept on a cheap and uncomfortable futon about five feet away from me. We were both in our twenties and needed privacy. Two, he wasn't willing to make the changes he needed to be a better roommate. I told him I was disappointed that my plans to help him didn't work out but that he'd have to move back in with our mom by the end of the month. Little did I know, this was the start of a petty dispute that would leave a lasting effect on my family dynamic more than a decade later.

Picking Sides and Playing Favorites

Did I mention that my brother is the favorite? My mom took the news as a personal attack. I was kicking out her baby boy. El consentido. *Instead* of staying neutral in a disagreement between two adult siblings, she picked sides. I felt like she sided with my brother and shamed me for "being a bad sister" and "not being there for family." She told me that if I sent my brother back, she'd take my car away.

The car she was referring to was my four-year-old Toyota Corolla. She'd bought it for me when I started my first part-time job at seventeen. Back then, my mom couldn't afford to buy me a car outright, but she knew I needed it to drive myself to work and school. At the time, she sat me down and told me she didn't have money to buy me a car, but she could finance one for me. This meant that if I agreed to cover the car payments and all other costs of car ownership, she could take out a car loan in her name, and the car would be mine. I was just a high school senior happy to get a car and gain some independence finally. I eagerly agreed.

A Big Price to Pay

To buy the car, she paid a $2,000 down payment to the car dealer. That day, she handed me the keys and all the financial responsibilities for the vehicle. For four and a half years, I paid *every single* car payment, insurance premium, registration fee, and maintenance cost—totaling over $20,000 (yes, I did the math). That's a lot of money for a young woman just embarking on adulthood.

The financial burden of car ownership weighed heavy on my shoulders. To meet my financial responsibilities, I worked all through college in the restaurant industry, working late shifts and juggling my full-time course load to manage these expenses on my own. Most of my paycheck went straight to my car payment and left little for me to enjoy. I never missed a payment or asked her for help. I had worked hard to hold up my end of our agreement and sacrificed so much to pay for this car.

And now, it felt incredibly unfair that all my hard work could be taken from me over a disagreement between me and her consentido. But since my mom was the legal owner, she was within her legal right to take the car away from me. I knew my mom well enough to know she wasn't bluffing. She doesn't make empty threats. She had every intention of taking the car away. (Looking back, I feel this is a form of financial abuse. Financial abuse is when a person intentionally manipulates, intimidates, or threatens someone by withholding money or other assets to gain control in a relationship.)

Feeling Desperate and Hopeless

My situation was only worsening. Not only was I dealing with the hurt and emotional toll of my family drama, but soon I was going to be carless too. How was I supposed to get to work every day? I needed the car to function as an adult. I used the car for my work commute, to buy groceries, and to go to doctor's appointments. In this day and age, the solution is easy. You just pull out your phone and order an Uber or a Lyft to get to where you need to go. But back then, ride-sharing apps didn't exist the way they do today.

I didn't have any family in LA, so it wasn't like I could borrow anyone's car or hitch a ride. I couldn't walk to work because it was too far. Public transportation in LA is not very efficient or reliable, so although it was an option, it was less than ideal.

I couldn't afford to buy another car. I had graduated from college only six months earlier. I had no money. I had no savings in the bank. I had so much student and credit card debt. I was stressed about what to do next and how I'd come up with the money to buy a new car. I didn't have any other family to turn to. I couldn't believe my own family was doing this to me and making my life more difficult. What was I supposed to do?

Using Credit During Times of Need

After venting to a good friend, he encouraged me to go to the car dealer and apply for a car loan. He was savvy with money and said that even though I didn't have any savings, I might be able to qualify for a car loan with no down payment with the income of my new full-time job. I was skeptical because this seemed too good to be true—a new car with no down payment? But I was desperate and figured I had nothing to lose.

I took his advice and went to the dealer later that week. After test-driving several cars, I hesitantly applied for a car loan. I crossed my fingers and toes and hoped for some good news in the midst of my debilitating family drama. I desperately needed this car.

A few minutes later, the car salesperson cheerfully shared that I'd been approved on the spot! And because of my good credit, not only did I qualify for a $0 down payment, but I also qualified for 0 percent interest which meant I could finance the car without owing interest—which would save me tons of money over time.

I felt a wave of relief and comfort enter my body. I had a replacement car, and I didn't need to pay a large down payment for it. I didn't have to lose any more sleep over my car drama anymore. My problem was fixed. I drove away from the car dealer with my new car that same night, thankful to have found a solution to this awful nightmare. My good credit had just saved my ass!

My brother moved out later that month, and as a welcome back home gift—guess who was given my four-year-old Corolla?

Using Credit to Your Advantage

I made a lot of poor money choices as a young adult. Since nobody taught me how money worked, I didn't prioritize an emergency fund which led me to feel trapped in a toxic workplace that caused me to burn out. My debt was out of control and made me feel helpless and stressed when living with awful roommates. But I didn't realize that in the background, I was managing credit responsibly and building a strong credit score.

My brother and I have made up since our family drama, but the experience taught me good credit is a lifeboat when you have nothing else. If you're ever in a rough spot, I want credit to do the same for you.

What is a credit score?

Think of your credit score as a report card. On this report card, you get graded for how responsible you are with paying back the debt you've borrowed.

Your credit report is compiled by three companies called credit bureaus. The three major players are Equifax, Experian, and TransUnion. A credit score can range anywhere from 300–850. Just like in school, the higher your grade, the better. A higher credit score shows lenders you can pay back your debt on time, which makes you a more attractive borrower. They do not like mala pagas.

As we discussed in the last chapter, lenders don't loan money out of the kindness of their hearts. They lend money because it's a business to them, and they can make money off you. And loaning money to people who aren't going to pay it back is just bad business. A credit score is what they use to determine whether they can trust you enough to loan you money.

Why You Need Credit

Credit is the fourth pillar in my First Gen Five framework because a good credit score gives you options and flexibility. Privileged Patty and Average Amy can get financial support from family to help them navigate big purchases. Since our immigrant parents come from more limited means and can't provide that type of support, it's important to take advantage of all the good that having a healthy credit score can offer to us.

Additionally, it's very hard to operate within the US financial system with no credit history. Here are some of the different ways credit affects your personal life:

- **Housing:** "I want to rent my property to a tenant who won't pay me on time," said no landlord ever! All landlords or rental companies will run your credit report as part of your application process to determine whether they want to rent a unit to you. If you want to buy a home, you'll likely need to borrow money to buy one. Purchasing a home costs thousands of dollars, and a mortgage covers the gap between your down payment and the listing price of the house. To borrow money for a mortgage, you'll need at least a 620 credit score. If your score is below 620, you may be denied a loan or pay a much higher interest rate as a penalty.

- **Big purchases:** Just like I needed credit to find a solution to the car drama with my family, you'll likely need credit to make similar large purchases. A car costs tens of thousands of dollars, so unless you have cash ready to use, you'll need to apply for an auto loan. Other big purchases you might need credit for are buying a mattress for your first apartment or buying an expensive electronic, like a laptop for school. Having a good credit score makes it easier to afford these necessities.

- **Loans:** Do you have plans to start a business one day? Starting a business from scratch will require a financial investment. You have to spend money to make money. Let's say you have plans to open a restaurant. You'll need money to pay for the lease on the building, kitchen equipment, food supplies, and point-of-sale software just to get started. A business loan can help you cover a lot of these up-front costs, but you'll need a good credit score to be approved for one.

- **Car insurance:** Underwriting companies use a variety of factors to determine your car insurance premium. They consider your driving history and whether you've had any car accidents, your occupation, and your age and gender, to name a few. One of those factors is your credit score. Since your credit score is your report card on how responsible you are with debt, they use that as an indicator of how responsible you'd be as a driver. The lower your credit score, the riskier a driver they perceive you to be, which means they'll charge you a higher car insurance premium. A poor credit score costs you more money. On the topic of cars, you'll also need a credit card to rent a car. You can technically rent a car without one, but it will usually require a cash deposit.

- **Employment eligibility:** This one may surprise you, but depending on your industry, it may be a common practice for your employer to check your credit score as part of the hiring process. As a former financial professional, every employer I've worked at has checked my credit score before hiring me. Since a lot of financial jobs give employees access to privileged financial information, they don't want to hire someone with severe money problems. They figure that if you're desperate for money, you may be at higher risk of doing something shady like stealing from the company or fudging some numbers to have money routed to your account. This also happens in the military. The military runs credit checks on their service members for high-clearance jobs. If a service member is strapped for cash, what's to stop them from accepting a bribe to sell military secrets to a foreign enemy? The military doesn't take those kinds of risks, so a strong credit score is required for high authority roles. A poor credit score can limit your career opportunities.

Busting Myths About Credit

Before we get into the specifics of how to build credit, we'll first have to clear out some misinformation you may have heard about credit. The Latine culture can be very cash-heavy. The "cash is king" ideology is rooted in the mistrust of financial systems and wanting to stay under the radar, both themes we covered in Chapter 2.

My dad only makes purchases with cash and avoids using credit cards. To him, cash is straightforward—you either have it or you don't. There are no weird formulas, interest to pay, or statement balances to decipher. If you have enough money to buy something all-cash, it's seen as a badge of honor, a signal that you can truly afford it. "¡Compro el carro al contado!" they proudly share. It's almost like cash is seen as safer and smarter to use.

Here are two of the most common misconceptions I see about credit cards and building credit:

MYTH: USING CREDIT CARDS WILL GET YOU INTO DEBT. YOU SHOULD JUST USE CASH.

Truth: Misusing *credit cards will get you into debt.*

A lot of people are scared to go anywhere near credit cards because they're afraid they'll automatically get into debt. I hear this often from students in my group workshops. This fear usually comes from a lack of confidence and lack of education on how to use credit cards correctly and responsibly.

A common reason people get into credit card debt is because they view credit cards as "free money." *It's not free money!* Remember, the lenders are expecting you to pay back every cent you borrow.

The key is to treat your credit card like *a debit card*. Do you run wild and go on a limitless shopping spree with your debit card? No, because you rein in your spending and know you only have as much to spend as there is in your checking account. If you did, you'd be consistently overdrafting or having your card declined for insufficient funds. Similarly, a credit card should only be used to make purchases you can pay off fully at the end of the month.

Although paying in cash is a guaranteed way to avoid debt, you can't build credit by strictly using cash. Credit bureaus need to see a track record of how you handle loans, credit lines, and debt. Additionally, using up large sums of cash instead of taking advantage of low interest debt is not the wisest use of that money. The smarter money move would be to *borrow* the low interest debt and use the cash to *invest* and grow your wealth, either in the stock market, real estate, or a business. Sometimes "safer" isn't always financially savvy.

MYTH: OWING A BALANCE ON YOUR CREDIT CARD WILL HELP YOU BUILD YOUR CREDIT.

Truth: Owing a balance is not required to build credit.

This one makes me want to pull my curly hair out. I'm not sure who made this one up, but I hear it a lot from my social media community which means somebody must be going around spreading lies. *You do not need to owe a balance to build credit.* Credit is built according to five specific factors that make up your credit score (more on that later in this chapter). Owing a balance is not one of them.

Carrying a balance is when you don't pay off the full balance of your credit card bill. Let's say you got #influenced to buy a walking pad after seeing all the girlies brag about theirs on TikTok. Who doesn't want to get their steps in while they're in a mindless Zoom meeting? The walking pad costs you $400, and you buy it with your credit card. Instead of paying off the entire $400 balance, some people think you should only pay a portion of it and leave the rest outstanding to build a good credit score. **This is the opposite of handling credit cards responsibly.** This is how you get into debt!

Since you didn't pay off the entire amount you charged to your credit card, you now owe the credit card company interest. Always pay off the statement balance to avoid paying interest charges. If you can't afford to pay it off fully, then consider putting off the purchase for a later date when you have the means.

Benefits of Having Good Credit and Additional Protection

Earlier, we covered some of the ways you need credit to function as an independent adult in the US economic system. We also dispelled some of the common misconceptions that can be a barrier to you building credit. If I haven't convinced you yet, maybe learning about some of the sweet perks a good credit score can get you will serve as a good motivator.

Having credit is the bare minimum. The goal should be to have an excellent credit rating because when you have excellent credit, you have more options. And a Latina with options is an empowered Latina!

If you have **excellent** credit, meaning anything over 720, you may qualify for these extra perks:

BETTER DEALS AND LOAN TERMS

The higher your credit score, the better terms you'll receive. Your high score demonstrates to lenders that you are an A+ student at handling credit. You're perceived as more financially responsible than others with lower scores. They know that if they loan you money, there's a pretty darn good chance you'll fully pay them back. You're exactly the type of person they want to lend money to.

Better loan terms are good for you because it means it *costs you less* to borrow money, this way you'll save money and have more cash to spend on what really matters to you.

This is what happened with my car story. Because I had excellent credit, I didn't have to pay a down payment, and I got 0 percent financing which meant I didn't have to pay interest on the $20,000 car loan.

For comparison, let's say someone with a poor credit score was trying to buy the same $20,000 car. The average car loan annual percentage rate (APR) for someone with a poor credit score is 9.75 percent. This means that with a five-year car loan, this person would pay **$5,340 more for the same car** in interest charges. That's 26 percent of the total car loan! Just because of a bad credit rating.

Because of my good credit, I've even gotten a free month of rent and my moving deposit waived when applying to a new apartment complex. Moving is not cheap and can be one of life's biggest stressors. You have to pay for moving supplies, movers, a moving truck, overlapping rent, a rental deposit, and the first month's rent. Getting extra perks like no deposit and free rent can make moving less stressful and help simplify your life. It pays to have good credit!

BETTER PROTECTION

Using a credit card to make purchases will give you more protection than using a debit card. Credit cards typically have more favorable policies against fraud and identity theft. If you bought something and later found it had a defect, you can use the credit card's return protection to get a refund. If you feel a merchant didn't deliver on a service you paid for, you can use your credit card company's dispute resolution and let them deal with the problem.

They also tend to give you better customer service than your bank. Additionally, a lot of credit card companies will pay for your insurance deductible if you use their credit card to rent a vehicle and have a car accident. An insurance deductible can range between $500–$2,500, so that's extra peace of mind. That's just a few of the many perks available through credit cards. You can't get these kinds of benefits with your little old debit card.

REWARDS

Another great feature of credit cards is the ability to earn rewards. Rewards can come in the form of cash back, travel benefits, or points to buy merchandise, gift cards, or concert tickets, to name a few. Can you imagine going to a Karol G concert and sitting in the front row for free? Credit card rewards give you the ability to do that! I've traveled to Italy and back—all with travel rewards.

Before you get too excited, I do want to warn you that using credit card rewards is for the advanced credit card owner. It can be easy for a new user to overspend on a credit card in the name of earning more points. That's exactly why these credit card companies offer you these perks. They want you to overspend, get into debt, and owe them interest. The trick is beating them at their own game by having your spending in check and only charging what you can pay off at the end of the month. This way, you can rack up points without paying them any interest. If you want a list of my favorite travel rewards credit cards, download the C&C Resource Pack at culturaandcash.com.

BALANCE TRANSFER OFFERS

This is also an advanced strategy but very underrated and worth noting. A balance transfer offer is a great way to pay off credit card debt. This is how it works.

Let's say you have $5,000 in credit card debt with American Express with an APR of 24 percent. That high of an APR makes it hard to pay off your debt because, on top of paying the $5,000 balance, you also have to pay high interest for borrowing the money. It's hard to pay off the debt in those conditions.

Since you have a strong credit score, you get a letter in the mail from a different credit card company—let's pick Capital One—offering you a balance transfer offer. With the balance transfer offer, they're saying, "Hey, hun! We noticed you have $5,000 in credit card debt. How about you transfer the balance over to us, but instead of charging you 24 percent interest like those meanies at American Express, we'll charge you 0 percent APR for the next twenty-one months. What do you say?"

There's a big benefit in that 0 percent APR. It's an interest rate freeze, similar to the student loan interest pause the US Department of Education enacted during the pandemic for students who owed federal student debt. The promotional period allows you to make significant progress toward paying off the $5,000 while paying no interest charges. All the payments you make will be going *directly* toward eliminating the balance. The catch is that it's only zero interest for the promotional period, in this example, twenty-one months. After that, you go back to paying high-interest charges.

Think of it this way. We all know the story of Cinderella. Cinderella's fairy godmother cast a magic spell so she could attend the ball in a horse-drawn carriage and a beautiful sparkling ball gown. Her dress and everything else will go back to the way it was when the magic spell breaks at midnight.

Your promotional period is the magic spell. Be smart with it! It won't last forever. Take advantage of it and make extra payments to pay down your balance. In our example, the magic ends after twenty-one months.

If a balance transfer offer sounds appealing, keep in mind that they usually cost a flat 3 to 5 percent fee, which I think is worthwhile to get that interest freeze. Don't make any additional purchases with the new card and instead use the interest rate freeze to make all the extra payments you can toward paying off your balance. If you're ready to buckle down and pay down your debt, a balance transfer offer may be your solution!

When Using Your Credit Card Goes Bad

Now let's address the elephant in the room. Using credit cards responsibly can bring you a lot of benefits. You'll qualify for better deals and have more options, which ultimately means more money in your pocket.

But using credit cards irresponsibly can lead to credit card debt, and in Chapter 5, we already covered it's one of the worst kinds of debt you can have because of the high-interest rate. It can be easy to overspend money on a credit card, especially in today's day and age, where everyone on social media is seemingly living their best life.

Any time you open a social media app like TikTok or Instagram, you see people drinking their green smoothies in their aesthetic kitchens, overlooking a city view in their high-rise apartments, showing off their trendy #OOTD, and enjoying Instagrammable vacations. It's human nature to feel FOMO and think, "I work hard. I deserve this too!" and charge the money on a credit card against your better judgment. But the truth is you don't know how those strangers on social media are financing their lifestyle. They could be trust fund babies, have sugar daddies or sugar mamas, or be buried in credit card debt. Resist the urge to overspend and live outside of your means just because others are seemingly living a more lavish lifestyle.

Credit Card Red Flags

A large credit card debt balance can derail your finances, make it harder to reach your financial goals, can negatively affect your mental health, and possibly even result in bankruptcy.

Here are some red flags that demonstrate you're using credit cards irresponsibly:

- You're using your credit card to make all your purchases, including food, clothes, gas, dining out, and entertainment. There is no limit to what you use your credit card for.

- You're using the card to charge items you typically can't pay with your debit card, like exotic vacations or trendy clothes.

- You're unaware of how much you're charging on the credit card each month.

- You can't afford to pay off the statement balance.

- You're only paying the minimum payment due.

- You've maxed out your credit line and can no longer make additional purchases.

If you catch yourself doing any of these, *stop*. Any of the behaviors listed above demonstrate that you've lost control of your spending. At this point, continuing to use the credit card will cause you more damage than good. Some financial pundits will recommend drastic measures, like cutting the card in half or freezing them in a glass of water in your freezer. What's worked for me is putting the credit card away in a box in the deepest part of my closet. Create some type of barrier to stop using it, and focus on paying off the balance you've accumulated.

Credit card debt is now at a record high. According to TransUnion, the average American carries $5,733 in credit card debt.[1] I've had my own battles with credit card debt. A couple of years ago, I went through a difficult breakup with my first serious boyfriend. Instead of coping with the breakup in a healthy way, I resorted to retail therapy. I went overboard shopping for new home decor to make myself feel better (BTW, it didn't help). I knew I didn't have enough money in my checking account to pay the charges off, but I figured future me could worry about that later. As I mentioned in the last chapter, sometimes our overspending is more emotional than logical. Before I knew it, I had $7,000 in credit card debt from my new shopping habit. I had lost control of my spending. Not only was I heartbroken, but now I was also in deep credit card debt. No man is worth that. Especially his dusty ass!

Credit Card Green Flags

To contrast, let's talk about some green flags that signal you're using credit cards responsibly:

- You're intentionally using credit cards. You only use your credit card for one or two spending categories, like groceries or gas.

- You only make purchases you can afford to pay off entirely at the end of the month. If you charge $1,000, you pay off the full $1,000 when your bill is due. You treat your credit card the same way you treat your debit card.

---

1   DeVon, Cheyenne. "Americans Owe Nearly $1 Trillion in Credit Card Debt—Here's the Breakdown by Age." Make It, June 9, 2023. https://www.cnbc.com/2023/06/09/how-much-credit-card-debt-americans-hold-by-age.html.

- You have a clear understanding of how much you charge to your credit card each month. The amount from month to month doesn't vary much.

- You always pay off the statement balance because you understand that paying off the statement balance will prevent you from paying interest charges and accumulating debt.

- You never make minimum payments.

- The majority of your credit line is still available to you.

Credit card debt can happen to any of us. According to the Federal Reserve Bank, Americans hold nearly $988 billion in credit card debt. There's something about swiping a shiny plastic card that doesn't make the money feel real. And with online shopping, ni se diga. Spending is just a click away; no swiping is even required anymore. Amazon's Buy Now button was strategically designed to get you to spend mindlessly. There are fewer opportunities for you to change your mind when a purchase can be made with a single click. But now that you've learned how to spot when you're misusing your credit card, you can identify when it's happening in real time and prevent burying yourself into a hole of credit card debt.

How Credit Scores Are Determined

Let's check in on what we've learned so far. We covered what credit is and why you need credit in the US. We also dispelled some common credit myths that can keep you from building a good credit rating. We learned some of the sweet perks you can get from having a strong credit score and how to spot red and green flags that demonstrate you're using credit responsibly.

Another reason people have a hard time building credit and managing credit cards responsibly is that they don't understand how their credit score is calculated. To build a good credit score, you first need to understand the formula credit bureaus use to calculate your score.

Here are the five factors that affect your credit score, in order of most important to least:

1. **(35%) On-time payments:** This is the biggest factor of the five and, in my opinion, the easiest to get right! Lenders want to see that you can pay your debt on time every single month. If you pay your bills late—even by a day or two— they see you as irresponsible and riskier to loan money to. When you forget to pay your bill on time, not only do you get slapped with a late payment fee (ranging between $25 and $40, depending on your credit card provider), but your credit score will also take a blow.

Luckily, this is very easy to avoid. If you set up auto pay on your account, your bill will be paid automatically. I'm a huge advocate of auto pay. Don't play yourself and say you'll remember to pay it every month. Life gets busy! Simplify your life by enrolling in auto pay and never miss an on-time payment again.

2. **(30%) How much you borrow:** The second biggest factor is how much money you *owe* versus how much money is *available* to you. Lenders want to see you use less than 30 percent of the credit available to you.

Let's walk through an example. Let's say you apply for a credit card and get approved with a $1,000 credit line. Most people will see that and think, "Sweet! I can charge up to $1,000 on this baby, and as long as I pay it all off, I'll be Gucci." Not so fast! The way the lenders see it, if you use all the credit available to you, you're a riskier borrower even if you pay off your balance in full. To them, it looks like you're going through money troubles. Remember, your goal is to look responsible and financially secure enough to pay back the debt owed. To stay on their good side and keep a healthy credit score, don't charge more than 30 percent of the credit available to you. In our example, no more than $300 should be charged on a $1,000 credit line.

3. **(15%) How long you've had credit:** The following three factors play a smaller role in your credit score, but they're still important to know. The next factor that affects your credit score is how long you've had credit. Lenders like to see a long, consistent history of someone being responsible with debt and credit cards.

This means that a forty-year-old who started working on their credit when they were twenty years old and now has a twenty-year credit history will have a higher score than a nineteen-year-old who's only been managing credit for a year. The longer you keep your credit line open and demonstrate you're being responsible with the money, the better.

4. **(10%) A variety of credit lines:** The fourth factor that affects your score is your credit mix. Lenders like to see that you're handling different types of debt responsibly.

Let's say Yesenia has four types of credit lines: She has a credit history that includes credit cards, car loans, student loans, and a mortgage. Now let's say Noemi only has one type of credit line: a car loan. And they're both equally responsible with repayment. Since lenders favor a varied credit mix, Yesenia would have a higher score than Noemi because she has a demonstrated history of successfully juggling different types of credit.

5. **(10%) How many new credit inquiries you have:** The last factor that affects your credit score is probably the trickiest of the five. Luckily, it only makes up a small percentage of your overall score. Basically, the credit bureaus punish you any time you do a credit check. When you apply for a new credit line, whether that's to open a new credit card or take out a car loan, lenders will process a "hard inquiry." A hard inquiry is when a lender formally pulls your credit report to decide whether they're going to loan you money or not. It's a part of their application process when you apply for a loan.

   A hard inquiry can also happen when you fill out a rental application to apply for a new apartment or when a credit check is required as a background check for a new job. Every hard inquiry dings your score, so be mindful of how often you process one. If you have too many hard inquiries all at once, the credit bureaus see that as red flags. They think, "Woah! This person is desperate to borrow money. Could they be going through some money problems? If they're strapped for cash, maybe there's a chance we won't get our money back, so this person isn't that trustworthy to loan money to right now."

I know. It seems counterintuitive, right? Penalizing someone applying for credit because they need the money. It's almost like that's the whole point. But you have to remember that lenders are not charities. The only reason they loan you money is because they intend to collect it back and make money from charging you interest. If they see financial chaos in the making, they want no part of it.

Gigi's Fool-Proof Way to Build Good Credit

Now if you're feeling overwhelmed by all the new information, I have good news for you. I have a hack to build good credit on autopilot! I created a simple, three-step process to simplify your finances and help you build a good credit score while you sleep. I taught this strategy to my younger brother Pablo when he turned eighteen, and by the time he was twenty-one, he had an excellent score!

Here are the three steps to follow:

1. **Only use your credit card for one small, flat, recurring bill:** Take a moment to think about your monthly expenses. Out of all your bills, do you have a small bill that stays the same month over month?

A good example of this would be something like your Apple Music or Hulu subscription. As of this writing, I pay around $20 a month for Hulu. The sweet spot is somewhere in the $10 to $50 range. My Hulu bill is consistently $20 a month. It won't change drastically from one month to the next if I watch more or less TV. They bill me once a month. It checks all three boxes.

Small: $20 (check!)

Flat: Always $20 (check!)

Recurring: $20 every month (and check!)

Once you've decided which bill to use, use your credit card to pay this expense. Do not use this credit card (or any other credit cards) for anything else. Charge all your other spending on your debit card.

2. **Set up auto pay with your credit card to pay this bill:** Continuing with our Hulu example, go to your Hulu account and set up auto pay with your credit card. This way, Hulu will charge your credit card every month with no effort from you.

3. **Set up auto pay for this credit card with your bank:** Since your credit card is being charged for this bill, go ahead and set up auto pay with your credit card company to automatically pay your credit card balance with your bank. Once auto pay is set up, you can set it and forget it.

WHY IT WORKS

Do you remember the two biggest factors that affect your credit score? The two factors are on-time payments (35 percent of your score) and how much money you owe versus how much is available to you (30 percent of your score). These two factors make up 65 percent of your credit score, so that means if you have these locked down, your credit score will be in pretty good shape.

The method works because, by setting up auto pay, you will always make on-time payments, no matter how busy life gets. And by restricting your credit card use only to pay a small, flat, recurring bill, you're borrowing much less money than what is available to you. A small streaming bill should be well below the 30 percent threshold preferred by lenders.

This hack is great for anybody looking to build credit for the first time or anyone who's lost their grip on credit card spending and wants to get back on track.

ACTIVITY: SET UP AUTO PAY FOR A SMALL, RECURRING CHARGE

Think of a small, flat, recurring bill you can use for this hack. Consider things like a subscription service (Disney+, Spotify, etc.), your internet bill, or your phone bill.

Once you've selected the expense, log in to your account, access the billing information, update it with your credit card, and set up auto pay.

Now access your credit card account online, enroll in auto pay, and automate a monthly payment for the full balance.

Remember: Don't charge anything else on this card, just the bill you're using for this hack. Give it a little time and watch your credit score soar!

How to Track Your Credit Score

Now that we've covered the five factors that make up your credit score and my three-step hack to build good credit, let's talk about the importance of regularly monitoring your credit score. To preserve a healthy rating, you'll have to track and monitor your credit activity. Here are several reasons why you should keep an eye on your credit score.

Staying on top of your score can help you detect fraud or identity theft as soon as it happens. Let's say you notice a sudden drop of fifty points. That's a big dip and should raise some flags if you haven't done anything out of the ordinary. After doing some research, you find the reason for the dip is because a new credit line was opened in the last month. But it turns out you didn't open this credit line. Someone else did! This means your Social Security number has been compromised, and you may have been a victim of identity theft. The sooner you take action and report the fraudulent activity to the credit bureaus, the better.

Regularly reviewing your credit report will also help you make sure the information lenders see is accurate and up-to-date. If you do catch any mistakes, they may take some time to be corrected. And you don't want incorrect information to work against you at a time when you need credit.

Monitoring your score also allows you to have a clear picture of your credit position. The goal is to understand how you're doing and what you can do better. You don't want to have any surprises when applying for a new loan or credit line. You should know where you stand well before you apply for a loan.

Tracking your credit score doesn't have to be another daunting task on your to-do list. Here are two easy ways to track your score:

1. **Request a free credit report:** As a consumer, you're entitled to one free credit report from all three major credit reporting

agencies once a year. Ordering your credit report does not hurt your score. You can request your free annual copy from AnnualCreditReport.com. Once you have your credit report, review it in detail to make sure you don't see any inaccurate information. The goal is to verify that all the information on the report can be tied back to you and not to someone else who compromised your personal information. Because these scammers be scammin'! You can also access your credit score for free and sign up for monthly notifications with credit-karma.com and quizzle.com.

Pro tip: Set up a yearly calendar reminder on your phone so you remember to practice these steps and stay on top of your credit score.

2. **Credit tracking apps and websites:** There are lots of free websites and apps on the market that can help you track your credit score. Some of the popular ones are Credit Karma, CreditWise, Experian, and myFICO. Almost all credit card companies these days offer free credit monitoring as part of your benefits. Once you opt to receive this free service, you'll be able to view your credit score in real time anytime you log into the app or website. You'll also get access to free educational resources to learn how to maintain a healthy score.

Navigating Credit with the Familia

Now that you've learned all the benefits of credit let's talk about how to navigate credit with your family. The interesting thing about being a part of a collectivist family is that when people know you have good credit, you'll instantly be the go-to person if a financial need comes up. In this section, we'll discuss what to consider when loaning out your credit and how you can help a younger member of your family improve their credit score by becoming an authorized user.

What to Consider When Loaning Your Credit

My friend Rafa has a good cautionary tale of his experience loaning his credit to family. His dad really wanted to purchase a $2,000 TV but didn't have the money or credit for it. He asked Rafa to finance it for him and assured him he'd pay him back. Rafa was happy to help his dad and trusted that he'd repay him, so he charged the TV purchase on his personal credit card. They agreed his dad would make all payments and would pay it off within two years.

But a few months later, his dad started skipping payments. Rafa would notice the bill was unpaid, and he'd ask his dad for an explanation. His dad would tell him he had some unexpected expenses that month and that he wouldn't be able to make the payment. Rafa understood that if payments weren't made, it would ultimately affect his credit score, not his dad's, so he started paying the bill out of his own money. He started resenting his father for not holding up his end of the agreement, and it put a strain on their relationship. Looking back, he regrets loaning out his credit for a TV and wishes he would have said no when asked.

Out of the First Gen Five pillars, loaning out your credit is the one that can cause the biggest financial entanglement. If you decide to loan your credit out, understand that your credit score is affected if payments aren't made on time. If the person you're taking out the loan for stops paying, you'd be responsible for paying.

Consider whether you have the financial means to pay for this in the event it happens. If you can't afford the payments, the debt will run delinquent and will negatively affect your credit score for years. This can affect you later down the line when you're ready to buy your first home or need to finance an auto loan. You'll also need to consider whether this situation could cause a rift in the relationship between you and the borrower. If you think it could and the relationship is important to you, it might be wiser to turn down the request, even if it is family.

There are other ways you can offer support. You can make the time to teach them what you've learned about credit in this book and show them how to build good credit on their own. Their credit score won't be fixed overnight, but at least you're empowering them to develop stronger credit managing skills for the future.

Setting Up Your Familia with Good Credit

If you have a good credit score and know a family member who could use some help building credit, consider adding them to your credit card line as an "authorized user." An authorized user is someone who's been added to the primary credit card holder's credit line. The authorized user has their own credit card assigned to them and is able to make purchases on their account, just like you are.

This is how it works. Let's say you have a fifteen-year-old teenage sister, and as the older adult sister, you want to hook her up with an early start to building credit. You'd contact your credit card company, either online or over the phone, to add your sister to your credit line. They'll need her personal information, like her name, date of birth, Social Security number—all that fun stuff—to add her to your account. Some credit card companies do this for free. Others charge a fee, so make sure to review the details with your credit card company.

Once they've been added, keep using your credit card responsibly, and with time, your sister will benefit from your good credit.

That's it! She doesn't actually need to be swiping the card for purchases for her to benefit from this hack. It's like piggybacking off your good credit.

You can technically give her the physical credit card, as she is an authorized user. But I personally wouldn't. I don't trust teenagers, and I don't have the time to babysit them. I remember what I was like at that age, and I would have definitely run off on a shopping spree with my friends the moment I got the chance. Teenagers do teenage things.

If you decide to hand over the card to your authorized user, understand that you'll be responsible for all charges made to your account. Any mishandling of the credit card ultimately affects the credit score of the primary cardholder, a.k.a. you. The point in adding her as an authorized user is to do her a favor, not to create more headaches for yourself. You're better off keeping the extra credit card in your possession and letting her ride along with your good credit history.

By using this strategy, you'll help your younger sister build credit while she's a minor, and by the time she turns eighteen, she'll already have a head start with her credit rating. Her record will show an established credit history, which will help boost her credit score, give her better lending rates, and save her money. This is how you set up those you love for financial success.

A Healthy Credit Score Has Your Back

In this chapter, we focused on credit and all the good that comes with having a strong credit rating. We learned how our credit score affects the type of housing, loans, and even jobs we have access to. We debunked some common credit myths that may be preventing you from using credit cards more wisely. We also covered the additional perks you can get from having good credit, like qualifying for better loan terms that save you money or earning rewards on everyday spending. You now understand what red and green flags to look for to check if you're using your credit cards responsibly. We learned the five factors that make up your credit score and how my three-step hack can help you improve your credit rating on autopilot. Lastly, we covered how you can monitor your credit to keep the scammers at bay and what to consider when letting your family use your credit line.

Managing credit doesn't have to feel scary. Now that you've learned what affects your credit score, be mindful of your credit card usage and adjust your spending behavior when it's gone unchecked. Out of the other pillars in the First Gen Five, building credit is the easiest and quickest to implement. Saving for a peace of mind fund and eliminating debt can take years. Budgeting and intentional spending is a daily practice. In the following chapter, we'll learn it can take decades to reap the benefits of investing in the stock market. But by practicing your new credit skills, you may see a noticeable improvement in your credit score within a year. And with my credit hack, you can do it with very little effort.

We're almost at the end of this book. You should feel very proud of how far you've made it and all that you've learned along the way. In our last chapter, we'll focus on long-term investing, the last pillar in the First Gen Five. Investing in the stock market can feel a little daunting if you're a beginner. But don't worry. I'll keep the concepts simple and easy to understand. By the end of the chapter, you'll have the knowledge and confidence you need to start investing and become the first stock market investor in your family.

CHAPTER 7

INVESTING ISN'T JUST FOR PATAGONIA-VEST-WEARING, MIDDLE-AGED, WHITE MEN

Every day I am becoming richer.

We've spent the majority of this book talking about the financial steps you can take to set yourself up for a bright financial future. Like making sure you have a healthy peace of mind fund to ditch a toxic work environment and protect your mental health, and building a spending plan tailored to your unique values allowing you to achieve your dreams and life goals. Creating a plan to eliminate debt so you have more space and freedom to use your money toward what you love—and lastly, hacking your credit score so you can create more flexibility for yourself when you need it and earn extra perks and cash savings.

But what if none of that mattered? Let's pretend you're rich and money isn't an issue. What would you do if money was abundant? If you had enough money to cover all your living needs and then some, *what would you do with your time if you didn't have to work for money?*

Would you spend more time with family, like cooking with your parents and enjoying longer visits without feeling the pressure of getting back home to wake up early for work the next day? Maybe you'd spend more time traveling and immersing yourself in new cultures without having a stack of paperwork waiting for you at your desk once you get back. Or if you've always wanted to learn how to play the guitar, maybe you'd spend your time taking guitar lessons and practicing your new instrument at home. If you enjoy your job, maybe you'd still work but only on a part-time basis, because although you find your career fulfilling, you don't need to work full-time for money anymore. You'd be showing up to work because you want to, *not because you have to*. Take a moment to dream about what life would look like if you had complete control to design an everyday life that prioritizes your needs, values, and passions. Really think about it.

Amigui, you've just gotten your first taste of what financial freedom looks like! When you're financially free, it means you have enough income or wealth not to have to work again. You can work if you want to—or not! You are work *optional*. You get to design what your mornings, afternoons, and evenings look like. You're no longer bound to a boss or corporate politics, or performance reviews. You are truly free to craft the life you want to live.

But how does one become financially free? There are a couple of ways to do it:

- You can be born rich.

- You can marry rich.

- You can win the lottery.

- . . . Or you can invest!

What is investing?

When you invest, you use money to buy assets and plan to sell them in the future for a higher value than you bought them for. It's how you make your money "work for you." For example, nobody buys a house for $300,000 and hopes that one day they can sell it for less at $50,000. The point is for your asset to grow in value over time and to sell it for *more* than you bought it for. Some common ways people invest are by buying real estate, investing in a business, or investing in the stock market.

Out of these three, stock market investing has the lowest barrier to entry. This means that for First Gen wealth builders who come from lower financial means, it's the easiest to access. With real estate investing, you'll have to research the best rental market to be a landlord in, and you'll need thousands of dollars for a down payment to buy a property. To invest in a business, you'll need to devote long hours to start your new business venture and may even need a hefty business loan. With stock market investing, you can start with as low as $10 a month and basic investment knowledge. This chapter will focus on investing for your financial future by using the stock market.

I have to admit, the former investment professional inside me is geeking out with excitement to start this chapter. I love teaching this topic and can write an entire book on investing. Since investing is only one of the five pillars of my First Gen Five framework, my goal in this chapter is to teach you the basics of investing. I'll help you overcome any mindset blocks that keep you from taking action, educate you on why investing is necessary for First Gen wealth builders, and provide some beginner-friendly tips to get started investing now.

What the eff is the stock market?

In the same way that Amazon is a marketplace to buy anything from electronics to furniture to clothes, the stock market is a marketplace to buy financial instruments, like stocks, bonds, and mutual funds. Stick with me, and don't be intimidated by the fancy words. At this level, you don't need to know exactly what these things mean, just that they are investments available for purchase in this marketplace called the stock market. For now, think of the stock market as a place where you can buy a little piece of a company.

Let's use Rare Beauty as an example. In case you don't know, Rare Beauty is a makeup company by Selena Gomez. People love their highly pigmented blush, and I personally am a big fan of their prime and set mist. It smells so delicious! Even though Selena is the face and founder of the brand, she is not the only investor in Rare Beauty. Besides using her own funds to start the company, she also uses money from other private investors and bank loans to finance the business's needs.

Let's say Rare Beauty wants to expand and create a new product line for nail polish, Rare Beauty Nails. To launch, they'll need extra cash to conduct market research, develop the product, spend on advertising, and hire a new team. They'll need more money. Expanding a business is not cheap.

Instead of going back to the same investors or asking the bank for another loan, they could list Rare Beauty on the stock market. Once a company is listed on the stock market, it's available for the public to invest in it as well. When a company is publicly traded, everyday people like you and me can buy ownership of that company. If you own stock in Rare Beauty and the company does well, so do you.

As a stock market investor, your goal is to build an investment portfolio, meaning a collection of investments, that generates enough income to replace your salary. As the businesses you invest in grow, so do your profits. By investing in the stock market, you are essentially piggybacking off the success of those companies.

Once your salary is replaced by the value of your investments, you can say ¡hasta nunca! to your crappy boss and live off your investments. You no longer have to show up to work to earn a living. Your money is making money, and you've achieved financial freedom.

Common Investing Myths

I know learning stock market investing can feel very daunting, especially when you didn't grow up in a household that taught you stock market basics like the Privileged Pattys of the world. But in your lifetime, you've probably heard something about investing and compound interest from a math teacher or maybe from someone at work. You've heard of this elusive concept of investing and seen the stock market in the news and know it has *something* to do with money but don't understand what it does. As an adult, you may have been told it's "smart" to invest but have no clue how to take the first step and get started. Or maybe you do know the basics but haven't gotten started because you're stuck.

Before we cover how to invest, it's important to spend some time clearing out some common misconceptions you may have about investing.

MYTH: INVESTING SEEMS COMPLICATED AND STRESSFUL. YOU SHOULD ONLY INVEST IF YOU'RE AN EXPERT.

Truth: Investing is only as difficult as you want it to be. You do not need to be an expert to start investing.

This is probably the #1 objection I hear about investing when I teach Investing 101 workshops. We tend to fear the unknown and what we don't understand, especially if our money is at stake. It doesn't help that investing is packed with financial jargon, with terms like bear market, dividends, yield curves, and commodity trading. Hearing these foreign words can feel as intimidating as hearing a new language and not understanding it. It's natural to feel "I don't know what this means, and I feel dumb when asking, so this is not for me. Byeee!" To add to it, you probably see a lot of headlines in the news saying the stock market is tanking one day—sell, sell, sell! And the next day, it's recovered—buy, buy, buy! On social media, you scroll and get mixed messages about crypto, meme stocks, and NFTs. They all promise you you'll get rich quickly, but which can you actually trust?

Can investing be difficult, stressful, and risky? Absolutely! But does it have to be? Not at all. The complexity and risk all depend on your style of investing and what types of investments you choose.

The type of investing I do is very hands-off and low-stress. As much as I love talking about money, even I have better things to do with my time than keeping up with the latest stock market news and reading the newest financial forecasts. My investing style involves very little effort, which frees up my time to do things I really love, like chilling on the couch and rewatching vintage episodes of *The Real Housewives of Potomac*.

You don't need to have expert knowledge to start investing. The key is to *start*, even while you are just learning.

Think of it this way. Let's say you want to start an exercise routine. Do you need to research the best exercise techniques to get the most intense workout? No, you don't need to be a personal trainer or an Olympian to start exercising. All you need to do is just start by doing something simple like going for a jog or doing a YouTube workout at home.

We don't need to overcomplicate things. As you start feeling more confident about your exercise routine, you can start learning new workout techniques to meet your fitness goals and take it to the next level. The same is true for investing. Just start and learn as you go.

MYTH: INVESTING IS ONLY FOR THE RICH.

Truth: Investing is for everyone, regardless of income.

It's easy to feel like investing isn't for us when we didn't grow up in a family of investors. My parents aren't stock market investors, and neither are my grandparents or my ancestors before them. When was the last time you saw Hollywood come out with a movie showing a Latina lead as a successful Wall Street investor? Instead, we see douchebag bros swallowing goldfish in the middle of a trading floor in *The Wolf of Wall Street.* No wonder it doesn't feel like it's for us. We don't see this representation at home or in the media, so it's only natural to feel it's not for us.

But investing is for everyone, no matter your income! Of course, investing is much easier for the rich. But you don't need large sums of money to start investing. You can start investing with something as small as $20 a month and work your way up. That's the cost of your Netflix account. You can afford that! Once you have more money available to you, you can always bump that number up, but the key is to get started while you are young so that you get into the habit of investing and give your money more time to compound and grow. More about this in a bit.

MYTH: YOU SHOULD ONLY INVEST ONCE YOU'RE DEBT FREE.

Truth: You can balance investing while actively paying down debt.

Many new investors falsely believe they'll make more money if they invest more money. They figure that since they have debt, they should pay it off first, and once more money is available to them, they'll be free to invest.

But the biggest factor that affects how much your money grows in the stock market is not *how much* you invest but *how long* you invest. The longer your money is invested, the more time it has to grow over and over again.

If I had waited until I was debt free to start investing, I wouldn't have started until my late twenties when I became debt free. I started earning a full-time salary at twenty-one, so I would have missed out on almost ten years of growth. You can never get those years back.

Now *how much* you focus on investing depends on what type of debt you have. Here is a good rule of thumb to follow. If you have high-interest debt, anything over 5 percent (like credit cards or car loans), then you're typically better off if you use extra cash toward making bigger payments on your debt and using minimal cash toward investing.

If you have low-interest debt (like student loans), then you're typically better off if you use extra cash toward investing more money in the stock market and making the minimum payments on your debt.

Here's a quick breakdown for reference:

If your debt is	>5% APR	Focus on debt but invest minimally until the debt is paid off
If your debt is	<5% APR	Pay minimum payments on debt and invest extra money in the stock market

But what if you lose your money?

Now that we debunked some common investing myths, let's talk about a common fear that keeps people stuck—the fear of losing money if the stock market crashes. You may have heard horror stories of the stock market crash during the Great Depression and the Great Recession. These two events financially devastated American families. It's a valid concern. Nobody wants to invest money just to lose it. But there's more to the story.

Let's take a quick history lesson on the stock market. Although there have been lows in the stock market, if you look at its history in the last 100 years, you'll notice that overall, the stock market tends to recover over the long term and go up in value. Check out the chart below:

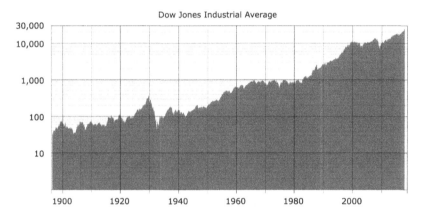

Dow Jones Industrial Average

Disclaimer: Past performance is not indicative of future results.

This chart represents the Dow Jones Industrial Average. Some people simply refer to it as "the Dow." The Dow is a way to measure the stock market's performance as a whole. It's a commonly used barometer of the US economy. This chart represents the Dow's performance for the last 100 years. The chart has plenty of ups and downs, especially during the Great Depression in 1929 and the Great Recession in 2008.

Can you lose your money in the stock market? You can, especially if you panic and cash out your money when the market's down. But look at the chart and notice that over the long term, the stock market goes up. In fact, in the last 100 years, the stock market has averaged an annual return of 9.81 percent.[1] That means that if you stick with it and give it time to recover, it tends to go up in value over time.

This chart shows that American businesses as a whole are resilient and tend to overcome challenges, even through the ups and downs. Remember, investing in the stock market is investing in businesses. And the goal of a business is to grow and profit over time.

However, this doesn't guarantee that the stock market will always recover though. There is no such thing as guaranteed returns. Just because it's recovered in the past, it doesn't guarantee it will always recover in the future. But hopefully, seeing the stock market's history will help you overcome the fear and misconception that investing is just a losing game. Its past recoveries should give you faith that it can repeat the process and do it again.

Or think of it this way. If investing in the stock market was just a money pit where everyone lost their fortune all the time, do you think the rich would still use it? Of course not. These people have access to the best financial minds and all the resources to invest in *anything* they want. Their goal is to *grow* their money, not to set it on fire. If they felt there was a better way to use their money, they wouldn't bother with the stock market! But they do because they understand that the stock market is designed to grow in value over time. Rich people like to stay rich.

Be Wary of Well-Intentioned Bad Advice

Now let's talk a little about something I like to call "well-intentioned bad advice." Another obstacle you may come across is discouragement from your immigrant parents.

---

1   "Stock Market Returns Between 1928 and 2022," S&P 500, https://www.officialdata.org/us/stocks/s-p-500/1928?amount=100&endYear=2022.

When I started learning about investing, I was so excited to tell them everything I was learning about the stock market, the magic of compound interest, and how it could be used to build wealth and achieve financial security. Instead of being celebrated for making smarter money moves and becoming the first stock market investor in the family, I was actively discouraged from investing.

My parents said, "But why don't you buy a house instead? It's the best investment you'll ever make!" Para empezar, they aren't mutually exclusive. You can invest in the stock market *and* buy a home. You don't have to pick one or the other.

But most importantly, buying a home to live in is not an investment. Unless the home is actively making you money, like a rental property would, the home you live in is not an investment.

I understand where my parents are coming from. When you don't have a lot, you don't want to risk the little you have. They were just trying to look out for me. They don't have the financial knowledge that I do, so to them, investing in the stock market seems risky, and buying a home seems like a safer bet. They feel this way because a home is something they can see, feel, and touch. It's tangible. The stock market is not. But don't let someone's fear, even if it is your parents', hold you back from starting your investing journey.

Why You Need to Invest

Let's check in and do a quick recap of what we've covered in this chapter. We learned that investing has the power to buy you financial independence and that the stock market is just a marketplace to invest in growing businesses. We dispelled some of the most common investing myths and covered why you shouldn't live in fear of a stock market crash. Lastly, we learned to tune out well-intentioned bad advice from those we love.

Now let's discuss why investing is absolutely necessary, especially as a First Gen wealth builder.

THE LATINA PAY GAP

According to LeanIn.org, the average Latina earns 54¢ for every $1 a white, non-Hispanic man makes.[2] Because of this pay gap, Latinas stand to lose at least $1,000,000 over the course of a lifetime. While we work on a solution to systemically close the pay gap, we can take advantage of investing to help us bridge the wealth gap.

NOBODY WANTS TO WORK UNTIL THEY DIE

Do you want to work until you die? I don't even want to work right now, and I'm thirty-four years old! I can't imagine what it must feel like to be eighty-plus years old, your body feeling countless years of working, and still having to show up to work. But unfortunately, this is a reality for a lot of people because either they didn't prioritize planning for their retirement or didn't have the financial means or knowledge to build a nest egg.

I watched my seventy-five-year-old grandfather return to work after suffering a stroke because he couldn't afford to retire. I don't want that to be me. I don't want to stress about money when I'm older. After working the majority of my adult life, I want to have a dignified retirement and enjoy the fruits of my labor. I want to spend the last phase of my life surrounded by those I love and doing the hobbies I find fulfilling, not working in a cubicle under fluorescent lighting at a nine-to-five to pay the bills.

---

2   "Latinas Aren't Paid Fairly—And That's Just the Tip of the Iceberg: Get the Facts about the Pay Gap for Latinas." Lean In. Accessed July 13, 2023. https://leanin.org/data-about-the-gender-pay-gap-for-latinas#!

Investing creates a stream of income that replaces your salary, so you don't have to spend your aging years working for a paycheck. And since US Latinas have the second longest life expectancy for women, you want to be financially prepared.[3]

SOCIAL SECURITY ISN'T GOING TO CUT IT

A common misconception is that Social Security is supposed to act as your retirement plan. Every time you earn a paycheck, your pay stub shows a deduction for Social Security taxes. Some people figure the government is collecting this money now to store it in a big metal safe with their name on it. Once they retire, they think they can knock on the government's door and ask them to open that safe and hand over their money. But that's not how it works!

The Social Security taxes you pay now are used to pay the benefits of current retirees. It does not go into a fund for you to use in the future. When you're old and gray, your Social Security benefits will be paid by younger people who are actively working. The younger generation pays for the benefits of the older, retired generation.

The problem with that model is that the US population isn't growing like it used to. According to the CDC's National Center for Health Statistics, data collected showed a sharp decline in fertility rates. American families are having fewer kids, which means the workforce will be smaller, and the Social Security pool will shrink in size. As of right now, Social Security reserves are projected to run out by 2037.[4] Which means that if you plan to retire after the

---

3 Castañeda, Laura, "Latina Longevity Is Real, but It Can Bring Health, Financial Challenges," NBC News, July 11, 2019, https://www.nbcnews.com/news/latino/latina-longevity-real-so-are-health-financial-challenges-come-aging-n1015256.

4 Gross, Stephen C. "The Future Financial Status of the Social Security Program." Social Security Administration 70, (2010). Accessed June 26, 2023. https://www.ssa.gov/policy/docs/ssb/v70n3/v70n3p111.html.

year 2037, expect to receive less money than what Boomers are getting now.

Lastly, Social Security was never created to be our retirement plan. It was only created to be supplemental to our own retirement fund and to replace only 25 percent of your income. Can you live off 25 percent of your income? I sure can't. That means you should plan to bridge the gap now through your own retirement investing.

YOUR EMPLOYER WON'T RETIRE YOU, EITHER

But wouldn't your employer help you with retirement? Before, they did through what are called pensions. This is how a pension works. You work at a company for a set period of time, usually twenty-five to thirty-five years. After those years of service, your employer would reward your loyalty by providing you with guaranteed income for the rest of your life.

The problem is that today only 4 percent of private sector employers offer pensions, down from 60 percent in the early 1980s.[5] Unless you work for the government, odds are you probably aren't entitled to a pension, which means you're on your own to secure a dignified retirement.

RETIREMENT ISN'T AN AGE, IT'S A NUMBER

Are you bummed to hear that pensions and Social Security won't be enough? Don't be! I remember when I first learned about this, I thought, "So I have to plan for my own retirement when other generations got fat pensions?! That's not fair! The Boomers ruin everything!"

---

5   "Ultimate Guide to Retirement: Just How Common Are Defined Benefit Plans?" CNN Money. https://money.cnn.com/retirement/guide/pensions_basics.moneymag/index7.htm.

But this is actually more liberating than you may think. With the old model, employees *had* to work twenty-five to thirty-five years to qualify for their pension and to retire. This is why when you think of the typical retiree, you picture an older, gray-haired person in their sixties.

But now that retirement is left completely to us, that also means we get to decide *when* we retire. There is no law that says you need to wait until your sixties to retire. We don't have to wait thirty years like other generations did. This means you can retire in your fifties, forties, or even your thirties. It all depends on how much money you invest.

Because retirement isn't an age, it's a number. So that means as soon as you have the financial means to retire, you can! I find this incredibly motivating to prioritize retirement investing. It can be hard to get excited about retirement investing when it feels like it's decades and decades away. But what if you could retire in ten or fifteen years?

These are the teachings of the FI/RE community, which stands for financial independence, retire early. It's a movement where people save aggressively toward retirement to reclaim their time and retire well before the traditional retirement age of sixty-five. This topic is outside of the scope of this book, but if you're curious, look into it and see if it's for you. The FI/RE movement fueled me with inspiration to take charge of my finances.

GENERATIONAL WEALTH? WE DON'T KNOW HER!

Another reason investing is absolutely necessary for First Gen is that we don't have the luxury of generational wealth. Privileged Pattys and Average Amys can chill. They're going to have their parents, and maybe even their grandparents, set them up financially by paying for college or contributing to a down payment on a home. Or they'll receive an inheritance when someone in their family kicks the bucket. We don't have that. We have to create that foundation for not just ourselves but for future generations and for our parents who didn't have the financial means to prioritize their finances. There is no future life raft coming to us. We either create it for ourselves, or we don't have it at all.

COMPOUND INTEREST—GIVE YOUR MONEY A JOB

And now to a much more exciting reason why you should invest— to earn compound interest! Albert Einstein famously called compound interest "the eighth wonder of the world," and for good reason.[6] It's honestly like magic. Compound interest is when your money makes money. When your money is invested in the stock market, it can grow through compound interest. This can best be explained in the chart below:

	MONTHLY CONTRIBUTION	LIFETIME CONTRIBUTIONS	AFTER 40 YEARS	COMPOUND INTEREST EARNED
Marisol starts at age 25	$300	$144,000	$1,593,333.20	$1,499,333.20
Fernanda starts at age 35	$300	$108,000	$592,178.48	$484,178.48

*Marisol has earned almost 3 times as much assuming a 10 percent rate of return

This chart shows two investors, Marisol and Fernanda.

6   Backman, Maurie. "Einstein Said Compound Interest Is the 8th Wonder of the World. Why Graham Stephan Thinks That's Right." The Ascent: A Motley Fool Service. January 5, 2023. https://www.fool.com/the-ascent/buying-stocks/articles/einstein-said-compound-interest-is-the-8th-wonder-of-the-world-why-graham-stephan-thinks-thats-right/.

Marisol started investing at the age of twenty-five. She invested $300 a month for forty years until she retired at sixty-five. Her money compounds over and over again from age twenty-five to sixty-five. By the time she's sixty-five, Marisol has built an investment portfolio of $1.5 million—while only adding $144,000 of her own money (assuming a 10 percent annual rate of return). Her money is making money. Brava, Marisol!

Now let's look at Fernanda's investing journey. Fernanda thought she had to be completely debt free before she could start investing, and she didn't start until age 35 once all her student debt was paid off. She invested the same $300 a month for the next thirty years. Over her lifetime, she added $108,000 of her own money, and by the time she retired at 65, she had built an investment portfolio of only $592,000.

She contributed only $36,000 less than Marisol did, but Marisol's early start earned her $1 million more in compound interest. $1 million more! This example shows the real power of compound interest. With compound interest, your money grows over and over again the sooner you start and the longer you invest. Lesson here: it pays to start early!

STILL NOT CONVINCED?

How did Marisol make almost ten times her investment while Fernanda made only five times her investment when their contribution was only a $36,000 difference? It's not proportional. It's like the math ain't mathin', right? But the reason Marisol's investment is bigger is because she got started *earlier*. As we discussed before, the biggest factor that affects how much your money grows in the stock market is **time**. *This is because compound interest isn't linear. It's exponential.*

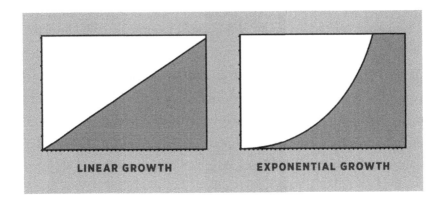

LINEAR GROWTH   EXPONENTIAL GROWTH

The money doesn't grow in a straight, steady, and predictable line. It rockets up in a curve. This means the earlier you start investing, the more time your money has to compound over and over again, and the harder your money works for you. That's why you have to start ASAP, to let compound interest do the heavy lifting. You work hard, and so should your money!

INFLATION IS A SILENT KILLER

Another mathematical reason why you have to invest is because of inflation. Inflation is when the costs of goods go up over time, which reduces your purchasing power. Did you know a Hershey's chocolate bar used to cost 5¢ in the 1950s? That same bar costs $1.59 today. That's inflation at work. Over time, it costs you more money to buy the same things.

The topic of inflation has previously been a little challenging to teach to my financial literacy students. It can seem like an abstract concept. But a lot of Americans felt the real pinch of inflation during the COVID-19 pandemic. Now it costs significantly more money to buy a car, groceries, or housing than it did prior to the pandemic.

Inflation negatively affects our finances because it slowly eats away at the value of our money. This means that a dollar today won't have the same buying power in the future. Our money is worth less if we just let it sit. Since investing can make your money grow, it's necessary to keep up and beat the effects of inflation.

How to Start Investing

Now that we've covered what investing is, debunked common myths, and explained why you need to invest—especially as a First Gen wealth builder—let's talk about how you can start investing.

When people first hear about investing in the stock market, they think their first move is to choose what stocks to invest in. "Okay, I'm in, Gigi! Should I buy stock in Disney, Starbucks, or Tesla? Which company will I get the most value from? Where do I begin to research?" But these decisions are actually further along in the process. First, let's start with step 1.

STEP 1: OPEN AN INVESTMENT ACCOUNT

To start investing, the first step is to open an investment account. You can't buy shares of Apple with your checking or savings account. You'll need to open an investment account that gives you access to the stock market.

There are many types of investment accounts to consider, including brokerage accounts, 401(k)s, 403(b)s, SEP IRAs, and Roth IRAs, just to name a few. We'll cover some of these in a moment. But all these accounts fall into two buckets: tax-advantaged and taxable.

Tax-Advantaged

Tax-advantaged accounts give you tax breaks. Nobody has ever said, "I'd like to pay more taxes, please!" This means you can delay paying taxes or can pay taxes now and not worry about a future tax bill.

The tax-advantaged accounts we'll cover below were created to help with retirement investing, which means you will pay penalties and heavy taxes if you use the money before retirement age or for anything other than retirement (there are exceptions—check the IRS website for specifics).

Why do you think the government gives you tax breaks if you invest for retirement? Because they care about us? Of course not! The government does it to incentivize us to create our own nest egg. They don't want to have to deal with a bunch of broke, aged-out-of-the-workforce seniors in the future. If we fail to plan for our own retirement, we'll rely more heavily on social and government-funded programs, which is a bigger headache for them. They get ahead of it by throwing us peasants a bone and giving us tax breaks to fund our own retirement. Take advantage of it!

Retirement Accounts

When deciding between tax-advantaged and taxable investment accounts, I'm a strong believer that First Gen wealth builders should start their investing journey through tax-advantaged accounts like their workplace retirement accounts. This would include a 401(k) or a 403(b). It's practical and simple to get started.

A 401(k) is a retirement plan offered to most private sector employees—ranging from law firms to grocery stores. A 403(b) is similar to a 401(k), though it's generally for education and non-profit employees. For simplicity, when I refer to 401(k)s in the rest of the chapter, I'm also including all workplace retirement accounts, like 403(b)s and 457 plans.

Here are some reasons a workplace retirement account (like your 401(k)) is the easiest way for you to start investing:

EASIEST TO START COMPARED TO OTHER ACCOUNTS

Signing up for your workplace 401(k) is easy. To start investing with your workplace retirement plan, all you have to do is sign up with HR. You'll have to fill out some forms saying you want to be a part of their existing plan and choose how much of your paycheck you want to contribute to the account every pay period. You can change this amount at any time if needed. No other setup is required to start. It's that simple!

With other investment accounts, like a Roth IRA or a brokerage account, you'll have to do a little more legwork. You'll have to do research to figure out the best broker to work with, open an account on your own, link your bank account, contribute money yourself, and sift through a myriad of investments. It doesn't take a rocket scientist to do any of this, but the more steps required, the more likely you are to throw your hands in the air and say, "Que hueva, I give up. This is too much." Fewer barriers to starting means you'll get started sooner.

AUTOMATIC CONTRIBUTIONS

Another benefit of using your workplace retirement account is that you're only able to add money to the account **automatically**. Every time you get paid, money is automatically deducted from your paycheck and sent straight to your account. You never see the money. And money you don't see is money you can't spend. So while you're busy doing life, your investment account is growing automatically every time you get paid.

EASIER TO PICK INVESTMENTS

More experienced investors will consider this a drawback of investing in a 401(k), but it's great for new investors just like you looking to get their feet wet! With a 401(k), you have limited investment options. Instead of having access to the entire stock market, you'll only be able to invest in the fifteen to twenty investments your employer preselected for you. If you had access to the thousands of securities available in the stock market, you'd easily feel overwhelmed by all the options, get stuck, and not pick anything at all. This is also known as choice overload. And you can't earn compound interest if you don't start. When it comes to beginner investing, having more options isn't always better.

EMPLOYER MATCH

And my favorite reason: an employer match! Many employers will incentivize you to contribute to your 401(k) with an employer match. Let's say your employer offers a 6 percent, dollar-for-dollar match, and you earn $50,000 a year. That means that if you contribute 6 percent of your income to your plan ($3,000), your employer will add an *additional* 6 percent ($3,000) of company money to your account.

This means that even though you only added $3,000 of your own money, you get a total of $6,000 added to your investment account! It's a great employee benefit, and you should make full use of it. A 401(k) match is a part of your compensation package, and if you don't take advantage of it, you are leaving money on the table. ¡Y tontas no somos! Ask your HR department if they offer an employee match on retirement contributions, and make sure to contribute *at least* enough to get the match.

Side note: Don't just stop at the match. If you can afford to squirrel away more than the match, please do. I used to have a cheap-ass employer who only offered a 3 percent match. Since they only matched 3 percent, I only added 3 percent of my own money and thought I was killing it. Kris Jenner who? But looking back, adding a total of 6 percent toward retirement is not the flex I thought it was. Most financial experts recommend at least 15 percent to have a dignified retirement. Contributing to the match is the bare minimum. If it's all you can afford now, that's okay, and there is no shame in that, but make it a goal to bump that up as soon as you have the means.

BUT WHAT IF YOU DON'T PLAN TO STAY AT YOUR EMPLOYER FOR LONG?

I see this question a lot in my social media comments section. Your decision to invest in your workplace retirement account shouldn't be affected by how long you plan to stay at that job.

Whether you work at that job for six months or thirty years, any money that *you* contribute to the account is always *yours*. This means that if you added $20,000 to your account, all $20,000 are yours. The money is portable and can be transferred over to your new employer's plan.

However, you may not be allowed to keep the money your employer added as part of the employer match. That depends on what's allowed by your company's "vesting schedule." Every company has its own unique vesting schedule. Some plans let you keep your money from the very beginning, others after meeting a specific tenure. It varies—check in with your HR department to understand the applicable vesting schedule for your plan.

The Roth IRA

But what if your work doesn't offer you a workplace retirement plan, like a 401(k) or a 403(b)? Then consider opening a Roth IRA. Since you can't opt in with your employer, you'll have to put in a little more effort to set it up on your own, but the process can be fast and easy with the right instructions. Don't let this discourage you. You are capable of getting it done!

WHAT IS A ROTH IRA?

IRA stands for "individual retirement account," so think of it as a private retirement plan that has no ties whatsoever to your employer. A Roth IRA is not industry-specific, which means you can be a teacher or a hairdresser or a dog walker and still have an IRA as long as you qualify for one. Check IRS.gov to see the latest guidelines to make sure you qualify, and pay special attention to the income limits.

You can open an account as a substitute for not having a 401(k) available to you, but you can still have one *even if* you do have a 401(k) at your work (if you meet the income limits). If you can afford to add money to both accounts for retirement, you'll only thank yourself later. It will be more money for you to use in retirement. I have both types of accounts.

One of the biggest benefits of using a Roth IRA is that you don't pay taxes when you use the money in retirement. Nobody knows what future taxes will be. They could be lower than they are today, but if I had to guess, they'd probably be higher.

Remember that in our Social Security discussion, we mentioned Americans are having fewer kids? Fewer kids mean fewer taxpayers. And fewer taxpayers mean less money for the government to operate on. My Spidey senses tell me taxes will probably increase in the future. By using a Roth IRA, you pay taxes now and don't have to worry about future taxes for that account.

TAKE ADVANTAGE OF IT WHILE YOU CAN

You may not always qualify for a Roth IRA, which is why you should use one if you qualify now. Unlike a 401(k), a Roth IRA has income limits. This means that if you make too much money, you won't be able to use one, and you'll miss out on the tax benefits that make this investment account appealing to invest with.

Stick with me as I geek out on the tax benefits a little further. As of 2023, the IRS only allows you to contribute to a Roth IRA if you make $138,000 as a single filer or $218,000 as a married couple filing jointly. So if one day you're a badass jefa making $250,000 at your day job, you'll no longer qualify for a Roth IRA because you make more than the IRS threshold.

This is good for you. You're making great money! It's not a bad problem to have. But it will be a little tougher to contribute to a Roth IRA the easy way. There are tax strategies and loopholes to get around this, but they'll usually require the guidance of a seasoned tax professional. The key takeaway here is to take advantage of the account while it's easily available to you.

You can open a Roth IRA in less than fifteen minutes. The process is simple but requires some effort on your part. If you want to access an updated list of my favorite beginner-friendly brokerage firms to open a Roth IRA, visit culturaandcash.com to download the C&C Resource Pack.

Taxable Accounts

Remember I mentioned there are two types of tax treatments for investment accounts? We already covered *tax-advantaged* accounts. The 401(k) and Roth IRAs fall under the tax-advantaged category. Now let's explore *taxable* accounts.

A brokerage account is a taxable investment account. Brokerage accounts come with many benefits. They don't have any income or contribution limits which means a high-income earner making $800,000 a year can qualify and can add as much money as they want into the account. They're also not industry-specific, which means anyone in any industry can qualify for one.

TAXABLE ACCOUNTS CAN OFFER MORE FLEXIBILITY

In my opinion, the biggest benefit of having a brokerage account is that you can access your investment money *before* retirement age. You can access your money at any time. If you want to invest in the stock market but want to access your money before the age of fifty-nine years and a half, then a brokerage account is a great option.

Let's say you want to invest in the stock market to buy a vacation home in fifteen years. You can use a brokerage account to grow your wealth and access the money penalty-free at any time. It's a great tool to build long-term wealth without having it locked away for retirement.

UNDERSTAND THE TRADE-OFF

However, since a brokerage account is *taxable*, you won't have as many tax benefits as you did with the previous accounts we mentioned. As a First Gen wealth builder, your first priority should be securing your retirement, especially when it comes with tax benefits. Remember, most of us won't get to benefit from a hefty inheritance later in life, which means we need to lay that strong financial foundation for ourselves. This long-term goal is far more important than a short-term investment goal, which is why I don't recommend First Gen wealth builders start here.

Taxable accounts are worth mentioning because they're extremely popular on social media. Robinhood and Acorns have become synonymous with investing. Both are taxable investment accounts. Social media finance bros love hawking both these companies because they earn affiliate income when you open a Robinhood or Acorns account through their affiliate links. They can't make affiliate income off you investing in your 401(k).

They don't care about the tax consequences you'll face or whether a taxable investment account is suitable for where you are in your investing journey. All they care about is getting their bag. I've seen their videos and they're compelling. They convince you taxable accounts are the only way to invest, which may lead you to neglecting your not-as-sexy retirement account.

The smarter move would be to make use of your tax-advantaged accounts first. Once those accounts have been fully used, then you can graduate to a taxable brokerage account. Or you can utilize one sooner, as long as you understand the consequences and trade-offs.

	TAX-ADVANTAGED		TAXABLE
Account name	401K, 403B, ETC.	ROTH IRA, ROTH 401K	BROKERAGE ACCOUNT
Contributions	Tax free	Taxable	Taxable
Growth	Tax free	Tax free	Taxable
Withdrawals	Taxable	Tax free	Taxable
Can withdraw	In retirement	In retirement	Any time

Investing in Crypto and Life Insurance

In this chapter, we've spent a lot of time covering tax-advantaged investment accounts like 401(k)s and Roth IRAs. But I would be remiss if I didn't mention crypto and life insurance. Both crypto and life insurance are hot topics these days and get a lot of hype on social media, which is why it's important for you to understand my stance on the two.

WHAT IS CRYPTO?

In the most basic definition, crypto is a form of digital currency. Crypto lets you buy products and services with digital or virtual currency instead of using traditional currency like US Dollars (USD) or Mexican Pesos (MXN). You may be familiar with different types of crypto, like Bitcoin, Ethereum, or Dogecoin, to name a few. Crypto is considered an alternative asset because it's relatively new and not heavily regulated like other traditional assets like stocks and bonds that have existed for centuries.

If you're worried about investing being risky, crypto is not the right investment for you. Crypto is inherently risky. The legal and regulatory framework is still evolving, which makes crypto's value fluctuate drastically compared to other traditional assets. The value is influenced by supply and demand, media hype, and investor sentiment. Celebrities like Kim K, Snoop Dogg, and Tom Brady have all encouraged you to buy crypto. But what do *they* really know about it? Where did they get their master's in finance at? I'll wait.

A WARNING ABOUT CRYPTO

The value of crypto can be sky-high one week and in the dumps the next. Most beginner investors can get spooked by the drastic swings, so unless you can weather the harsh conditions, you're better off staying away from crypto altogether. Crypto bros and other crypto fanatics are very loud and will convince you to think otherwise. They persuaded a lot of people to dump all their savings into this alternative asset (including my twenty-one-year-old brother Pablo, who did it against my advice).

But investing that much money into a single investment is extremely risky. When it comes to investing, you never want to put all your eggs in one basket. Even the large institutional investors I used to work for, with millions and billions of dollars in their portfolio, would typically only invest about 5 percent of their money into alternative assets.

As First Gen wealth builders, we don't have the privilege of losing money as a lot of the crypto bros on Reddit do. You're better off focusing on my First Gen Five and using your money on practical things like paying down debt, saving for emergencies, and investing for retirement in a 401(k) or a Roth IRA.

Luckily, the crypto hype has *really* died down since the 2022 collapse of FTX, one of the largest cryptocurrency exchanges, when $8 billion in customer funds went missing. So much for going to the moon!

WHAT IS LIFE INSURANCE?

Warning—this one is a bit morbid to talk about, but it's still an important topic to discuss. Life insurance is a way to protect you and those you love in the event of an unforeseen death. Just like a car accident pays you money in case you crash your car, a life insurance policy pays you in case the insured person passes away. A life insurance policy can prevent you from having to resort to a GoFundMe campaign to raise money for unexpected funeral costs. If anybody is dependent on your income to pay their bills or to finance their everyday life—like your partner, children, or aging parents—then buying a life insurance policy is a smart choice.

UNDERSTAND THE DIFFERENCE BETWEEN TERM AND WHOLE LIFE INSURANCE

Generally speaking, there are two types of life insurance: term life insurance and whole life insurance.

Term life insurance covers you for a set term and has no investment component. For example, a twenty-year term life insurance policy will cover you in case of death for the twenty years that you hold the policy.

Whole life insurance covers you your whole life and *does* have an investment component.

Financial experts will argue until they're blue in the face about the best type of budgeting method or the best strategy to pay off debt, but one thing we can all agree on is that life insurance *should not* be viewed as an investment.

Whole life insurance is a lot more expensive than term life insurance (about five times more!), and the investment component typically performs poorly compared to the stock market. This means you'll get more bang for your buck if you invest your money yourself in the stock market instead. It's also marketed as a good product to avoid taxes, but it usually only makes sense for the ultrarich, a.k.a. the one-percenters of the world.

A WARNING ABOUT LIFE INSURANCE AGENTS

Lastly, I'ma keep it real. Life insurance sales agents make a great commission from selling whole life insurance to you.

When I was in college, I interned at a life insurance company (don't judge me, I was just a kid trying to get a little professional experience). First, they lure you in with a free financial checkup. In their sales pitch, they'll tell you that buying whole life insurance is a smart investment because it's what rich people use, so you should too!

And they are correct. Some rich people *do* buy whole life insurance . . . *after* they've invested in tax-advantaged accounts, taxable accounts, real estate, businesses, rare art, collector vehicles, and everything else rich people have the resources to invest in. It's just one of the many things they invest in, but not all they invest in.

Again, whole life insurance usually only makes sense for the ultrawealthy. If it's not term life insurance, then it probably doesn't make sense for a First Gen wealth builder.

Investing with the Familia in Mind

One of my favorite things about teaching investing is showing others the power it can have for young children. Whether you plan to have children, already have some escuincles of your own, or just want to be the fabulous rich auntie, this section is for you.

Remember, the most important factor of compound interest is **time**. And what's one thing all kids have? Time! They have the rest of their lives ahead of them. If you start investing for a child when they're young, they have the benefit of letting that money grow over and over from the time they are a child and reach adulthood.

Here are some basics of the four investment accounts you should consider if you're looking to invest for that special kid in your life:

529

A 529 plan is an investment account for college expenses. It helps cover tuition, books, and room and board. According to Bankrate, on average tuition tends to increase by 8 percent per year.[7] This means that in twenty years, a year of higher education at a public school—including tuition, fees, and room and board—could average out to $54,000 a year. If you want to help future generations avoid student debt, a 529 account can be a great way to secure their future.

---

7   https://www.bankrate.com/loans/student-loans/college-tuition-inflation/

CUSTODIAL ROTH IRA

Similar to the Roth IRA, a custodial Roth IRA is an investment account for retirement. If an underage child works and has taxable earned income, they qualify for a custodial Roth IRA. But don't get creative here. A lot of people try to game the system and say their four-year-old "works" and cleans their office for $6,000 a year. Would anybody else hire your four-year-old to clean their office? Of course not. These kinds of ploys are like sending the IRS a personal invitation to audit you. If the child has a legitimate job, like a part-time gig at a local pizzeria, then a custodial Roth IRA might make sense.

UTMA/UGMA

First, a little bit about the acronyms: UTMA stands for Uniform Transfers to Minors Act, and UGMA stands for Uniform Gifts to Minors Act. These types of accounts give you the most flexibility relative to the other two we discussed. With a 529, the money has to be used for education, and with a custodial Roth IRA for retirement.

There is no specific use for a UTMA/UGMA. They can use the money for college expenses or use it to buy a new car. The IRS doesn't care. While the flexibility is hard to beat, there is one major drawback to using this type of account. Once the child turns eighteen, they are the legal owners of all the money in that account, so you'd need to feel comfortable knowing you have no legal say in how that money is used once the child is an adult.

BROKERAGE ACCOUNT

And lastly, you can open a brokerage account in your name, knowing the funds are to be gifted to the child in the future. The benefit of this type of account is that since the account is set up under your name, you have control over how much money the child will receive and when.

This is what I'm doing for my god niece, Samantha Baby. Samantha is three years old and has big curly hair like I do. As her nina and rich auntie, I set up a brokerage account the year she was born, and I add money to it every birthday and Christmas. My plan is to gift her the money once she's an adult. I love my baby niece, but if she's anything like my sister, she's going to be a des-madrosa at eighteen. And I don't feel comfortable giving so much money to an unknown eighteen-year-old version of Samantha. So, a brokerage account where I retain control makes the most sense for my situation.

If you're interested in leveraging any of these accounts, please consult a tax professional who can offer expert guidance.

FOR PARENTS

Now you may have been excited to learn about how compound interest can make your money work for you and how the special kids in your life stand to benefit the most from getting an early start. But what about your parents?

Our immigrant parents didn't have the privilege of learning about the US financial system. A lot of them may be behind in retirement planning or may not even have a retirement plan at all. According to Morningstar, only 8 percent of Hispanic households report having an IRA or similar retirement plan.[8]

---

8   Fox, Michelle. "Most Latinos Aren't Saving for Retirement, and Information Is a Big Factor: More than Two-Thirds of Hispanic Households Aren't Putting Aside Anything through Workplace Savings Vehicles Such as 401(k) Plans." NBC News, October 18, 2021. https://www.nbcnews.com/news/latino/latinos-arent-saving-retirement-information-big-factor-rcna3221.

I know that for a lot of us, planning for our parents' retirement is a big pain point. Not only do we have to make sure we pay down our debt, save for short-term emergencies, and invest for the future all on our own, but many of us also have to figure out how to come up with enough money to financially support our aging parents when they retire. I know firsthand the immense pressure one can feel from this responsibility. My dad has some real estate he'll use as his retirement income, but as the oldest of his children, I'll be expected to help him with unexpected medical expenses as they arise. I've already had to start planning for that.

I've also seen my aunts and uncles all chip in to financially support my grandparents, who left the workforce with no retirement savings or retirement income. One of my aunts has delayed her retirement and kept working so she can have enough money to send to my grandparents in México. As a collectivist culture, we're taught to take care of our viejitos like they took care of us when we were younger.

If you plan to help your parents with their retirement, and they have the financial means to contribute their own money toward it, here are some practical strategies to get started:

- **Consider workplace retirement first:** Have them check with their HR department to ask if they are eligible for a 401(k) or a 403(b) and if they offer an employer match. As I mentioned earlier, this path will require the least amount of set up, and if they're offered a match, you want to have them take advantage of this free money.

- **Consider an IRA:** If they aren't offered a workplace retirement plan, they may be eligible for an IRA like a Roth IRA or traditional IRA. If they are offered a workplace plan, they can still have a Roth IRA as long as they qualify for it. Visit

IRS.gov for the latest guidelines, as this information changes on a yearly basis.

- **Take advantage of catch-up contributions:** If your parents are fifty years or older, they will qualify for catch-up contributions. Catch-up contributions allow older employees to add more money to their retirement plans than younger employees. The idea is to give older employees an opportunity to make up for lost time and catch up as they are closer to retirement age. Visit IRS.gov for more.

If they don't have the financial means to contribute their own money toward retirement, or if you weren't able to convince them to invest in the stock market, try the following:

- **Help them reduce their spending:** To create more space to have extra money to use toward retirement, help them review their spending to check for any opportunities to cut down on unnecessary expenses. I recently found out my aunt was paying $150 a month on a storage unit she'd had so long she didn't even remember what was in it anymore! Cleaning out that storage unit and downsizing to a smaller unit could free up some cash she could use toward retirement.

- **Get them health insurance:** As your parents age, their medical expenses will increase. If they don't have health insurance, paying for their health insurance premiums is a smart way to avoid costly medical bills in the future and make sure they get the medical care they need.

- **Factor them into your budget:** Even after trimming down on expenses, some low-income parents still won't have the financial means to invest in retirement. If that's the case and you want to provide that financial support to them, have an honest conversation about what type of costs need to be covered. What expenses will they need help with? When they can no longer work for money, do they need help paying rent, utilities, and food costs? Work together as a family to understand what level of support will be needed and what you are able to provide. Add a line item to your budget to factor them into your spending and have regular money conversations about their retirement planning.

NORMALIZE NOT RETIRING YOUR PARENTS

And lastly, I've gotten comments in my comment section saying, "What if I don't want to retire my parents?"

As a financial educator, I've found there are typically three types of attitudes people have toward retiring their immigrant parents.

There are people who will retire their parents at all costs. Then, there are others who want to provide some level of financial support. And lastly, there are people who don't feel it's their responsibility to fund their parents' retirement.

If you don't have plans to help your parents with their retirement, that's okay, too. You are not a bad daughter because you choose to focus on your finances instead. Paying for someone's retirement other than your own is an immense responsibility and one that should only be done si quieres y puedes.

As discussed in Chapter 2, we all have our unique family dynamic and history, and we all get to decide what's in alignment with our values and best for our family and finances. It's a personal choice.

Earlier, I mentioned I'd be helping my dad with his retirement costs, but I won't be doing the same for my mom. And no, it's not because of the Corolla. The truth is she and I have a difficult relationship. We're estranged and haven't spoken in years. I wish it were different, but unfortunately it's not. After using the Quiero y Puedo approach I've decided to set the financial boundary instead.

If you've decided to do the same with your parents, my advice would be to communicate this decision to them. The cultural norm is for the adult child to financially support their parents in retirement, and you've decided it's not in your plans. That's okay. But you don't want them to assume they'll be receiving this aid from you and leave them completely unprepared.

Tell them up-front to give them time to prepare accordingly. Be transparent with them and share how you have other financial goals, and swinging both isn't in the cards for you. This may be a tough but necessary conversation to have. Be prepared to stand firm in your decision and your boundaries. Remember, you are not selfish for prioritizing your own needs. You're a bicultural Latina and are allowed to reject traditional values and expectations when they don't serve you.

If you're not able to financially support them, you can still offer help in the other ways I mentioned before, like by helping them craft a budget that creates room to build savings, reviewing their spending patterns to cut down on unnecessary expenses, and sharing knowledge about retirement accounts. Showing up for family doesn't come in one shape or size.

Chapter Recap

Phew! That was a lot. Let's do a high-level recap of what we learned in this chapter:

- Stock market investing is a tool we can use to achieve financial freedom and become work optional.

- Limiting beliefs or common misconceptions shouldn't hold us back from investing.

- Investing is absolutely necessary for First Gen because we don't receive generational wealth.

- Investing allows us to have a dignified retirement and beat inflation.

- Compound interest is the eighth wonder of the world and allows us to grow our wealth exponentially.

- The easiest way for First Gen to start investing in the stock market is through workplace retirement accounts (for example, 401(k), 403(b), 457 plan, etc.). You can opt in with HR at your employer.

- Contribute at least enough money to get an employer match if one is available. If you have the means to add more, do it.

- If a workplace retirement account isn't available, see if you qualify for an IRA (for example, Roth IRA, traditional IRA, SEP IRA, etc.).

- A brokerage account gives you the freedom to use the money before retirement but is taxed the most out of any other type of investment account.

- Don't invest in crypto unless you fully understand the risk involved.

- Whole life insurance policies typically only make sense for the one-percenters. Term life insurance is a smarter choice for most people.

- We can set up the next generation for financial success by investing in a 529, Custodial Roth IRA, UTMA/UGMA, or a taxable brokerage account.

- We can help our aging parents plan for retirement by help-ing them open investment accounts, taking advantage of catch-up contributions, trimming their spending, paying for their health insurance, and factoring them into our spending.

- If you decide you don't want to be responsible for your par-ents' retirement, be transparent with them and look for other non-financial ways to support them.

We learned a lot, but this is just the tip of the iceberg. As much as I'd love to geek out and teach you everything I know about investing, it's just not feasible in one book chapter.

My goal for this investing chapter is to help you overcome any limiting beliefs, help you understand the benefits of investing, and teach you how to get started. You don't start investing by thinking you should do it when you have more money or telling yourself you'll take it more seriously once you're further along in your career. You get started by opening an account. And now we are empowered with the knowledge to do that!

Next Steps

Once you've completed the first step and opened an account, you'll need to regularly add money to your investment accounts and select your investments. You'll also need to continue your financial education to become more knowledgeable and comfort-able with investing in the stock market. You'll need to learn how much money to invest, how to navigate your investment broker's website, and how to decide between investments such as stocks, bonds, REITs (real estate investment trusts), mutual funds, ETFs (exchange-traded funds), and more. Remember, opening an investment account is just the first step.

If you're ready to continue learning with me, I invite you to check out my self-paced online course called "Investing for First Gen Wealth Builders." The course includes twenty-plus on-demand videos that explain all these topics in detail, step-by-step video tutorials, and short quizzes to test your knowledge so you can jump-start your investing journey.

Scan this QR code to gain access now.

If you'd rather learn for free, my go-to personal finance websites are Investopedia.com, NerdWallet.com, and TheBalance.com. You can also borrow books from your local library. These two books helped me understand the stock market: *The Boglehead's Guide to Investing* and *The Simple Path to Wealth*. If you prefer to learn in person, look for free investing workshops hosted by nonprofits like the YWCA. Seek out the information and stay committed to your financial literacy journey. Keep at it, I'm rooting for you!

Investing is for you too!

By now, you should have a foundational understanding of investing in the stock market and should feel confident in your ability to begin your investing journey. Remember, you don't have to be a pro to start! Investing in the stock market will help your money grow and last longer because it's being put to work. Don't put off investing until "you know more" or "when you have more money." The biggest factor in how much your money will grow is time, and the time to start is now when you're young. I'm cheering you on as you become the first stock market investor in your family!

YOUR MONEY TRANSFORMATION AWAITS YOU

I can achieve what I truly desire.

A couple of years ago, I was hanging out at my friend Rebecca's childhood home. We were hanging out at her mom's house and chismeando about our high school memories. Being a little nosey, I started scanning her bedroom when I noticed she had a bookshelf full of personal development books. I asked her if I could borrow one, and she replied, "Take anything you want!" One of those books I borrowed was David Bach's *Smart Women Finish Rich*.

I'd read a few money books in the past, but none had touched me the way this one had. This one changed something inside me. It was the first book that made me realize that getting smart with money wasn't about having a big bank account you could brag about but about living a life that reflected what was truly important to you. That book inspired me to keep seeking more money books from different authors to learn about money from different points of view. It was the catalyst I needed to embark on my money journey.

Keep Learning the Language of Money

Although money is simple to learn, it's not intuitive. You have to be intentional with your education and seek out the information to feel more confident and build up your money management skills. As you move forward with your financial literacy journey, it's important that you continue learning in a way that speaks to you and keeps you motivated. I didn't learn from just reading one book. Read more personal finance books, especially from diverse authors you can relate to and that understand your unique money struggles.

Subscribe and listen to financial podcasts. Podcasts aren't your thing? Follow money content creators on social media that align with your values and share your lived experience on TikTok, YouTube, and Instagram. With the internet, it's easier than ever to have access to this information. Sign up for free financial newsletters. Register for a low-cost financial literacy class at your local community college. Check if your employer hosts financial education webinars as a workplace benefit. If they don't, petition them or collaborate with an employee resource group to bring it to your organization. Your girl is available for hire, just sayin'!

Be Proud of All You've Learned

By making it to the end of this book, you're already more prepared to tackle your finances and start living a life on your terms than when you started. This is something to be celebrated!

You learned that the First Gen starting line is different. Our lack of generational knowledge and generational wealth shouldn't discourage us from pursuing a life of financial freedom. Acknowledge that it's our reality. Our parents did the best they could with what they had. They brought us to this country to give us better opportunities and passed us the baton. And now it's our job to change the financial trajectory of future generations like they did when they bravely immigrated here.

We unpacked some of the additional barriers facing our community, like inheriting a scarcity mindset, the clashing of collectivist money values versus individualistic money values, and financial behaviors that keep us in the harmful paycheck-to-paycheck cycle. We covered how peace of mind funds can be used to help you exit relationships and rooms that aren't for you and how a values-based budget can help you achieve your financial goals without making you feel deprived.

We discussed how debt was a necessary evil for a lot of us but should be treated as a leaking faucet in your finances that needs immediate repair. You now understand how credit scores can be gamified in your favor and how a strong credit score can get you the best deals and save you the most money.

Lastly, we learned how investing is not a luxury only for the rich but a necessity for First Gen wealth builders responsible for our financial well-being and that of others.

Our Path Is Different but Not Impossible

The First Gen experience is different from your average middle-class family. When I started my money journey in my twenties, I had no idea how much my family, culture, and community would factor into my financial success. While others had the luxury of solely focusing on their own financial wellness, my money experience was always tied back to my family.

I shared several personal stories on how my bicultural identity affected my finances to humanize money and shed light on some challenges that may lie ahead in your journey. I hope it helps smooth out some bumps in the road for you. Only you can find the right balance for yourself and decide how you will honor your family, culture, and community while also prioritizing your individual needs. It's a different path, but you are strong, resilient, and so capable!

Plan Your Way to Financial Success

But all that you've learned won't matter unless you take action now. I would consider this book a failure if you read it and think, "This all sounds good, but I'll get to it later once I *insert an excuse here.*" I don't know a single person who wishes they'd taken their finances more seriously *later.* All the people I know regret not being more intentional with their money sooner. Right now is the time for you!

Remember, you don't have to know everything to get started. **You just have to start.** Start putting money aside for your peace of mind fund, even if it's just $50 a month. Use any extra income, like bonuses and tax refunds, to sock more money away. Try different budgeting methods and start tracking your spending to understand where your money is going. You won't have to do it forever, just long enough for you to get a good handle on your spending patterns. Anchor back to your "why," your reason for wanting to do all this in the first place. Get clear on your debt, and be intentional with paying it off. Hack your credit score so that you're building good credit on autopilot, and it's there for you when you need it the most. And contribute money to your retirement plans so you can have a comfortable and dignified retirement.

You'll make mistakes along the way, and that's okay. You may overspend on your budget or forget to pay a credit card bill. The key is to learn from the experience and do better next time. But keep going. You got this!

How to Financially Empower Our Comunidad

But most importantly, share the knowledge you're learning with your familia, amigas, and comunidad. More First Gen Latinas need to hear this message. Our money and our wealth matter, but it all starts with our education. I didn't start my financial literacy journey with an expensive course or a fancy degree. I started it by my good friend loaning me a free book from her childhood bedroom. Share this new knowledge as a tool to uplift our community and make an impact for generations to come.

Here are ten things you can do to spread financial awareness in the First Gen community:

1. Show your working-age younger sister the magic of compound interest with an online compound interest calculator and help her open a Roth IRA.

2. Teach your prima how to open a credit card line and show her how to hack her credit score.

3. Talk about money goals and dreams with amigas over brunch and chisme.

4. Explain the employer match at your company's 401(k) to your younger work bestie and encourage them to opt into the company plan.

5. Visit SSA.gov with your parents to calculate how much they'll receive in Social Security and start a conversation about retirement planning.

6. Work with your employee resource group leaders to set up financial wellness programming for your organization.

7. Write an Amazon review of this book. It will help me reach more women like you who need this message.

8. Start a virtual book club with friends to cover the topics in this book and other personal finance books.

9. Normalize money conversations with your family. Include them in your goal-planning process and share with them what you're excited to accomplish with your money.

10. Share your debt pay off wins on social media to inspire others to reach toward debt freedom.

You don't have to be a money know-it-all to make a difference. As long as you're a couple of steps ahead, that's good enough. By sharing what you've learned with others and normalizing these money conversations, you can help close the knowledge gap and transform the financial lives of others. You can be the catalyst in helping others build generational wealth and forever change the trajectory of their family!

From Flopping to Thriving

For the majority of this book, you've gotten to know a version of me that only exists in writing. I had to dig deep to relive the painful memories of my flop era and remember the stressful details to include them in this book. It was uncomfortable at times, but they're important money lessons to pass on to you.

Back then, I desperately counted the days until my next paycheck. I was buried in debt with no idea how to manage it or pay it off. I had no choice but to be stuck and deal with difficult roommates and toxic work environments. They all took a heavy toll on my mental health. I had no safety net or even a life raft. I had no awareness of my spending and overspent money to impress friends and family on stupid things that didn't actually matter. I was in constant conflict with my family over their money expectations and questioned whether I was a good daughter, granddaughter, and sister. It even had me question my *Latinidad*.

My financial anxiety kept me up late at night and made it difficult to live everyday life without being medicated. I didn't have the slightest clue about how to improve my financial situation. I felt completely helpless and was hardly scraping by with my money. Life was unnecessarily hard.

Today, I enjoy the soft life. I live in financial abundance and use money as a tool to enrich my life. My money doesn't control me or my mood. I control it. I built an eight-month FU fund that lets me leave spaces where I don't feel valued or safe. I have my spending down to a science and hardly rely on a budget because I'm clear on what's important to me and spend intuitively according to those values. I'm completely debt free, which creates more space to use my money on the financial goals that matter to me, like creating a savings fund to help my aging father with medical costs and investing in my niece's future. I have disposable income to spend freely on things that will make my life easier, like paying extra to have Instacart deliver my groceries so I can enjoy my Sunday evenings at home. When I had to take eight weeks off work to heal from an unexpected major surgery, I found comfort in knowing I had savings to float me through that unpaid time off. I take international vacations to Europe for free by taking advantage of credit card perks and without getting into debt by using a sinking fund. I invest aggressively in my retirement account and don't plan to work a day past the age of fifty because I'd rather spend my days enjoying my hobbies and family than hustling and grinding for a paycheck. And I created this financial security for myself while only making a modest salary of $70,000.

At this stage of my life, I live in harmony with my family. I clearly communicate my redefined money values and goals and lovingly set financial boundaries. I no longer tie my value and worth to my ability to be obedient and agreeable to my family's demands. I give money to them on my terms, not because I have to but *because I have the means* y porque me nace. Porque quiero y puedo.

The confidence I gained from building financial security allowed me to quit my safe corporate job to pursue my passion and teach financial literacy to young adults who look like me. I had the privilege to quit what my parents viewed as a pinnacle of success because I learned to master my money. I make a great living doing what I love while making a difference in the lives of others. The life I live now wouldn't have been possible if it weren't for financial literacy.

Now It's Your Turn

But I don't share any of this to brag or be a #bossbabe. My hope in sharing this is to show you that it's possible for you too. If you stay committed to your financial journey, this is the type of life you can create for yourself—even with a different starting line and no generational wealth. You *can* take control of your finances and make smarter money moves to design a life that truly makes you happy. By following the teachings in this book and my First Gen Five, you, too, can accomplish what I have and so much more. Put what you've learned to use, practice your affirmations, and seek support when you need it. I want you to move forward with confidence and excitement for your future. The soft life is waiting for you!

ACKNOWLEDGMENTS

Writing a book was nothing like I envisioned. I had pictured myself trying cute coffee shops all over Chicago. Spending hours getting lost in deep thought and writing. Maybe even making friends with the baristas or other patrons sitting near me and telling them all about my book. I even got excited about the possibility of finally fulfilling my traveling abroad dreams. Writing during the day and exploring my new surroundings in the evenings.

Because you can write a book from anywhere, right?

But the writing process was actually lonely, boring, and repetitive. As an ambivert and Leo who is naturally good at showing up on camera and connecting with others, I found writing to be a very isolating experience. I'm proud of myself for putting in the hard work and pushing through the challenges and self-doubt to meet one of my biggest life goals. Because I know this book will make an impact. I'm also thankful for those who supported me along the way.

First, I'd like to thank my husband, David, who turned into my unpaid book writing, book publishing, and book marketing consultant. Sweetie, I know you're just as happy as I am to have finally finished this book. Thank you for picking up the slack at home so I could focus my energy on writing. Thank you for being my rock and the person I could always turn to no matter what. I love you.

Next, my wonderful book coach, Stacy Ennis. Stacy, I know for a fact I would have never finished this book had I not enlisted your support. Thank you for caring about me, my reader, and my business. Thank you for helping me navigate the very archaic publishing process and encouraging me to hybrid publish. Thank you for being a friend and for helping me well beyond our coaching time together.

Thank you to Rachel and Lissette at Influence with Impact for handling all my brand work while I was focused on writing. I know that juggling my writing schedule and brand campaign timelines was like playing Tetris, but y'all did it well and made sure I was #paid. Special shoutout to my brand partners. You are my angel investors and made it possible for me to earn a living while writing. (Because ain't no book advance here!)

Thank you to TikTok, Macro, and UnbeliEVAble for awarding me the TikTok Latinx Creatives Grant. Thanks to your financial support, I was able to skip the two to three years it would have taken me to get this book to market with a traditional publisher. Your funding made it possible for me to write the book *I wanted* to write and that my reader needs. Not some whitewashed version palatable to a predominantly white publishing industry (79 percent if you're curious!). With your aid, I was able to hire my book coach and outsource the publishing process to a hybrid publisher, which allowed me to focus solely on my writing. I won't let you down and I'll pay it forward by uplifting others who come after me.

Thank you to my beta readers: Noemi, Violetta, Vicki, Ale, and Alexia. Your thoughtful feedback helped me edit out the cringiest parts of my manuscript. Thank you for keeping it real and telling me what I needed to hear. Your excitement for my book also gave me the boost I needed to keep going.

Thank you to the real-life Privileged Pattys, Average Amys, and First Gen Ginas for helping me shape my book back when it was only a concept. Long before TikTok, long before The First Gen Mentor, long before the grant, you all supported me with your time, transparency, and personal stories. You know who you are. I love you all!

Thank you to the entire team at Greenleaf Book Group for helping me make my vision a reality. It was comforting to know that I could work on other projects while a team of publishing pros was handling the production of the book behind the scenes. Special shoutout to Danny for believing in my concept from the beginning and to Jen and Lindsey for keeping my project on track. And to Jared, I absolutely love the book cover! Thanks for capturing my vision.

Thank you to my editors Johanie and Jon for being in the trenches with me and checking me when I had to be checked. Thank you for caring about my reader and for helping me enhance my message. I felt less alone thanks to you.

Thank you to Alyssa Gonzalez for the beautiful book illustrations. Your art is exactly what my reader needs to feel safe with my writing. Thanks for your hard work and for delivering on such a quick turnaround time.

Thank you to all the powerful and inspiring women who let me clout chase off their name and endorsed my book with an advanced praise. You are the embodiment of women supporting women! Thank you. Special shout out to Macro and UnbeliEVAble for helping me land the endorsement of my lifelong idol. The OG's know how much this means to me. Having Eva provide an advanced praise was not on my bingo card. I'm eternally grateful for your kindness.

Thank you to my social media community for cheering me on and keeping me motivated. I could feel your energy and excitement anytime I shared book updates either on socials or in my newsletter. Writing a book is the ultimate delayed gratification. I wrote it for almost a year with little feedback from anybody on how I was doing. But your sweet messages kept me going. Thank you.

And last but not least, I want to thank me. A la Snoop Dogg, I want to thank me for believing in me. For doing the work. For taking no days off. (JK I did take days off but sacrificed many weekends, holidays, and summertime Chi to meet writing deadlines). I'm proud of myself for working my ass off on my grant pitch and winning a $50k grant. I'm proud of myself for getting back on the horse after my hysterectomy. I'm proud of myself for putting the FOMO to the side and implementing the time boundaries I needed to get this book done. I'm glad I moved past a predatory and insulting book offer and a culturally insensitive editor who tried to whitewash my writing. I'm proud of myself for successfully juggling brand work and writing deadlines. I'm proud of myself for fiercely defending my vision, my reader, my communidad, and myself. Our stories need to be told *our way*.

I hope twenty-five-year-old Giovanna, who desperately needed this book, feels proud.

ABOUT THE AUTHOR

 **GIOVANNA "GIGI" GONZÁLEZ** is a financial educator, social media influencer, speaker, founder of The First Gen Mentor©, and a proud daughter of Mexican immigrants. During The Great Resignation, she quit her ten-year corporate career in financial services to pursue her true passion: teaching financial literacy to young adults.

Giovanna teaches personal finance and career navigation for First Gen at universities, ERGs, and other organizations and on her TikTok account @thefirstgenmentor. She was named a Top 25 Creator by *Fast Company*, 40 under 40 by the Hispanic Alliance for Career Enhancement, and "Latinx to Watch" by *Hispanic Executive*.

Giovanna has been featured in dozens of publications, including *The New York Times*, *Mitú*, and *Business Insider*.

She lives in Chicago with her spouse and their dog.

Visit her website at **www.thefirsgenmentor.com**
TikTok: https://www.tiktok.com/@thefirstgenmentor
LinkedIn: https://www.linkedin.com/in/giovannagonzalez/
Instagram: https://www.instagram.com/gigithefirstgenmentor/